JOHN WESLEY—CHRISTIAN CITIZEN

JOHN WESLEY—
CHRISTIAN CITIZEN

Selections from his Social Teaching

By

E. C. URWIN, M.A., B.D.

AND

DOUGLAS WOLLEN, M.A.

THE EPWORTH PRESS
(EDGAR C. BARTON)
25-35 CITY ROAD, LONDON, E.C.1

CONTENTS

FOREWORD

This small volume of *Selections from the Social Teaching of John Wesley* is offered as a contribution to the bi-centenary of May 24, 1738. In preparation for the celebrations of May 24, 1938, Methodists will be recalling with thankful hearts the great experience in which Methodism began. It was a Movement with two aspects—one turned inward to experience the love of God shed abroad in the heart, the other turned out to the world of men and human affairs. Others will write and speak at greater length of the first. Our task has been, starting from the first aspect, to direct attention to the second, in the hope that in the picture of Wesley the Citizen wrestling with the perplexities of his own age, we may at least find courage to face the distractions and bewilderments of ours, and so test the guidance a Christian man may derive from his faith in facing the tasks of citizenship.

We have tried also to serve a second purpose, namely, to make more easily available for general readers than hitherto they have been the social and political opinions to which Wesley gave such vigorous expression in the many pamphlets by which he sought to influence his day. These have often been made the subject of historical study and reflection by competent writers, but themselves remain buried in the large volumes of his works. It is our hope that this Selection will serve to interest a new generation in the many-sidedness of Wesley's influence.

Considerations of space have necessarily limited our selection. Some topics, like Wesley's views on Education and Health, have been omitted altogether, and we are very conscious that others might have chosen their selections more wisely than we have done. The task has afforded us keen interest, and we can but trust that we have not altogether failed to do it justice. It should be noted that in most cases we have preserved Wesley's peculiarities of grammar and spelling.

Further, the reader will find added help in the appreciation of Wesley as a citizen from reading the companion volume by our senior colleague, the Rev. Henry Carter, C.B.E., entitled: *The Methodist*.

E.C.U.
D.W.

INTRODUCTORY ESSAY

WESLEY AND THE EIGHTEENTH CENTURY

JOHN WESLEY, as Christian citizen, must obviously be portrayed against the background of eighteenth-century life in England, in which century also the religious movement he founded had its beginnings. It is a century which opens up some fascinating perspectives to the student. Wesley was born within fifteen years of the Revolution of 1688 which sent James II into exile; when he died in 1791 the French Revolution was well under way and the Reign of Terror was to startle Europe. As a boy he could talk with men who would remember the execution of Charles I; he was to live into the generation which saw the same fate befall Louis XVI of France. His early years were stirred with news of the victories of Marlborough; Prestonpans, which crushed the hopes of the Old Pretender, was fought when he was a lad of twelve, and his great ministry for England had barely started when Bonnie Prince Charlie made one last desperate effort for the Jacobite cause to see it crash in ruins at Culloden. We shall observe the nervous tension with which Wesley, as a Tory High Churchman, faced the Rebellion. There were circles in England in that day which regarded Jacobite and Tory as indistinguishable. Wesley might well think it necessary, in those Whiggish days, to make his loyalty to the Hanoverian succession perfectly plain.

Thereafter Wesley's days were spent, and the movement he founded grew, in the midst of political conflicts in which the actors were Walpole, Chatham, Wilkes, Junius, Lord North, Burke, Pitt, and Wilberforce. The stability of the throne, political as well as religious and civil liberty, the growth and meaning of empire, republicanism as a form of government, were subjects of debate almost throughout the century. The range of interests confronting the citizen was world-wide. It was the age of the French and Spanish wars, and the clash of arms resounded on the Heights of Abraham, the backwoods of America, the Straits of Gibraltar, and the plains of India. The American Colonies were lost, but compensation was afforded by the peaceful voyages and discoveries of Captain Cook, which gave Great Britain its first hold upon the island continent of Australia; and the issue of a brief, sharp struggle with Holland toward the end of the century brought her the dubious advantage of possession of South Africa.

These events gave to the English race a hold upon the greater part of the undeveloped portions of the globe. England ceased to be a Power whose position was determined by its place in a single continent; henceforth her destinies lay beyond the oceans! Wesley's conception of a world-wide mission was perhaps not un-influenced by this extension of British imperial power; at least it gave him his opportunity.

Equally, the latter half of the century resounded with the call of provocative and revolutionary social ideals. Questions of liberty and equality were thrown up by the agitations aroused by the Wilkes case, and fiercely debated in relation to the American War of Independence, and the French Revolution. The perpetuation of the wrong of slavery and the horrors of the slave trade became living issues of the day. Everywhere liberty was challenging privilege, and extending its claims to every relation of life, religious, civic and economic. The old social structure began to crack in every joint, and new conditions demanded new adjustments at every turn.

Finally, the closing years of the century saw the Enclosure Acts and the crowding of the dispossessed population into the towns. With new discoveries of coal and iron, and the invention of the steam engine, the Machine Age was born. At the beginning of the century, England was predominantly agricultural, nearly half the country was a waste of forest, moor, bog and fen, and outside London the population was concentrated in those counties like Worcestershire where the soil was most fertile. But towards the end of Wesley's lifetime all this was rapidly being changed. Population began to flow into the industrial regions of the North, gravitating around places like Manchester, Liverpool, Birmingham, Sheffield, Leeds, Bradford and Newcastle. England was becoming the workshop of the world, a new phenomenon in the social history of our race—the first industrialized State. The social consequences of this were stupendous; so vast, in fact, that it is not surprising that men were overwhelmed by them, or failed deplorably at first to subdue them to high social ends. Unexpected means of wealth were suddenly placed within their eager grasp, and opportunities for exploitation of human life and labour were well-nigh unrestrained. The new order of things added to rather than diminished the gulf dividing wealth from poverty, and already periods of depression, aggravated by war's grim aftermath, followed decades of prosperity. It was 'a revolution in which the older England . . . passed away for ever. A new England was born, at first misshapen, unconscious of herself and of her past; nor were there absent the usual pangs and pains of an unexpected birth'.

This was the world of political, economic and social change in which Wesley lived. How did he re-act to it? In the picture of

Wesley the leader of the Great Revival, which dominates our memory, the picture of Wesley the citizen is sometimes overlooked. Yet it is clear that while preaching the doctrines of the revival, calling men to Scriptural holiness and establishing the Methodist Societies were his supreme pre-occupations and the purpose for which he was called, he was very much alive to social and political issues of the time. He did not stand apart from the age nor aloof from the concerns of ordinary men, but was wide awake to all that went on about him. This alertness revealed itself in swift apprehension of the needs of the poor and oppressed, revolt from luxury, concern for social order, zeal for his country and loyalty to the King. Moreover, he was active in pursuit of these interests and in influencing his fellows to similar concern. By example and precept, he sought directly to influence public opinion. In an age of pamphleteers he was a prolific writer of these instruments of popular education in matters of politics and social righteousness, a voluminous letter-writer to the press, and on occasion from the pulpit a prophet of social righteousness. From such material, we shall endeavour to trace his activity in the sphere of politics and his influence on social conditions and the prevailing habits of the people. We shall let him, as far as possible, speak for himself, and by extracts from his *Journal*, letters and pamphlets, exhibit his constant solicitude for the poor, his doctrine of money, the changes he effected in social habits, and his attitude to successive events in the political sphere, from the '45 Rebellion and the John Wilkes case, to the American War of Independence and the Abolition of the Slave Trade.

Two questions will be before the reader. First, how far were Wesley's judgements as a citizen a direct result of his religion? Some of them, as his unceasing solicitude for the poor and his attitude to slavery, undoubtedly sprang directly from his sense of God's abounding love for all men. In others, we shall be conscious that he is influenced in his judgements by principles, convictions and prejudices inherited from his ancestry and stiffened by his Oxford training. A 'Tory High Churchman' is the true description of him in this connexion, and by this character his views concerning the nature of government, loyalty to the King, and religious, civil and political liberty were largely determined. From this standpoint, we can understand the judgements he formed on the issues in the Wilkes case and the American Secession War. Yet even here some change transpired. A High Churchman he ceased to be: a Tory he remained to the end.

Second, what guidance for the twentieth century can we glean from his example of eighteenth-century citizenship? No more than the history of one age can ever give to another. Wesley's supreme contribution to the world was the Evangelical Revival, not his citizenship. Nevertheless, with all its limitations, even this is instructive. For it shows us an alert Christian man applying his mind, heart and conscience to every part of life as he saw it, concerned for the well-being of his fellows, the stability of government, the integrity of public life and morals, and counting it part of his duty not only to exercise his judgement thereon but also to influence the opinion of others. Wesley was a power to be reckoned with, not only in the religious, but also in the political life of his times. And if to that influence there were limitations, and his judgement was sometimes fallible, as some would say in regard to his conceptions of political liberty or his views on the Secession of the American colonies, and if also there were problems he did not sight, then this also must be said, that this is just the side of life in which he knew judgement is prone to err from lack of knowledge and understanding. His views on the difficulties of judgement in politics are very sound. It is a particular illustration of the limits set to Christian Perfection. Perfect Love may control your temper, regulate your spirit, and inspire the motive from which you act. It cannot determine the truth of your judgements. That demands a hard discipline of the mind, and even the saints may err therein.

Yet something of his influence remains in the field of citizenship. His High Churchmanship is forgotten, but his repugnance to constitutional change and political agitation passed on to some of his followers in the days that followed when the fear of revolution was deep in Englishmen's hearts. Actually, however, it is at the points where his religion was most alive that his influence is greatest. His proclamation of the Gospel of the Grace of God for all, created a new self-respect in the humbler and despised industrial classes, made them sensitive to the claims of freedom and self-respect, and so regenerated their lives and characters that they became fitted to sustain great tasks of citizenship, and to bring to those tasks high vision and purpose. New impulses began to stir in the hearts of agricultural labourers, as at Tolpuddle, amongst Durham miners and the textile operatives of Lancashire and Yorkshire; and in the power of them great changes began to appear in the political, social and economic life of England. How far Wesley's own mind and heart, judgement and will, would have gone with these changes we cannot say, but it is not inconceivable that he whose heart went out to the poor, cared for prisoners and felt so sharply the wrong of slavery in the eighteenth century, would also have been stirred, as were many of his followers in the nineteenth century, by the concerns of social justice on behalf of those in his own land who were the victims of man's cruelty to man.

JOHN WESLEY—
CHRISTIAN CITIZEN

CHAPTER I

THE GREAT REVIVAL

Any account of the social teaching and influence of John Wesley must begin with the fact of the Evangelical Revival itself, the doctrines which inspired it and the transformations it produced in individual life and character. 'The experimental doctrines of the Evangelical Revival', says Dr. Rattenbury, 'are three in number: God's unqualified love for all mankind, the witness of the Spirit and Perfect Love.' The following quotations are intended briefly to recall the nature of the Revival that followed the preaching of these doctrines, and so greatly affected the life of England.

THE GREAT EXPERIENCE: MAY 24, 1738

I think it was about five this morning that I opened my Testament on those words: 'There are given unto us exceeding great and precious promises, even that ye should be partakers of the divine nature' (2 Pet. i. 4). Just as I went out I opened it again on those words: 'Thou art not far from the kingdom of God.' In the afternoon I was asked to go to St. Paul's. The anthem was, 'Out of the deep have I called unto thee, O Lord: Lord, hear my voice'.

In the evening I went very unwillingly to a society in Aldersgate Street, where one was reading Luther's preface to the *Epistle to the Romans*. About a quarter before nine, while he was describing the change which God works in the heart through faith in Christ, I felt my heart strangely warmed. I felt I did trust in Christ, Christ alone, for salvation; and an assurance was given me, that he had taken away *my* sins, even *mine*, and saved me from the law of sin and death.

I began to pray with all my might for those who had in a more especial manner despitefully used me and persecuted me. I then testified openly to all there what I now first felt in my heart. But it was not long before the enemy suggested, 'This cannot be faith; for where is the joy?' Then was I taught that peace and victory over sin are essential to faith in the Captain of our salvation; but that, as to the transports of joy that usually attend the beginning of it, especially in those who have mourned deeply, God sometimes giveth, sometimes withholdeth them, according to the counsels of His own will.

After my return home, I was much buffeted with temptations; but cried out, and they fled away. They returned again and again. I as often lifted up my eyes, and He 'sent me help from his holy place'. And herein I found the difference between this and my former state chiefly consisted. I was striving, yea, fighting with all my might under the law as well as under grace; but then I was sometimes, if not often, conquered; now, I was always conqueror.

Journal, Wednesday, May 24, 1738.

The Beginning of Field Preaching

At four in the afternoon, I submitted to be more vile, and proclaimed in the highways the glad tidings of salvation, speaking from a little eminence in a ground adjoining to the city to about three thousand people. The scripture on which I spoke was this (is it possible any one should be ignorant, that it is fulfilled in every true Minister of Christ?), 'The Spirit of the Lord is upon me, because he hath anointed me to preach the Gospel to the poor. He hath sent me to heal the broken-hearted; to preach deliverance to the captives, and recovery of sight to the blind; to set at liberty them that are bruised, to proclaim the acceptable year of the Lord'. *Journal, Monday, April* 2, 1739.

The Field Preacher at Work

What pictures, too, we get of the field preaching! The great hymn of invitation,

> All ye that pass by,
> To Jesus draw nigh:
> To you is it nothing that Jesus should die?

was obviously meant for the man in the street. One sees those surging throngs of hard-faced men and women, crowding to see a gentleman and clergyman, neat and dignified, standing in the open air and preaching. A man of Wesley's type arriving in an English village even to-day would arouse attention, for he was very different from the ordinary out-of-doors speaker, but in his day such 'enthusiasm' on the part of the Fellow of an Oxford college was unthinkable. The calm, firm voice announces the hymn and starts the tune. How startled the hearers must have been, who had heard no religious singing but psalms droned out unintelligently in church, to hear:

> Come, sinners, to the gospel feast,
> Let every soul be Jesu's guest;
> Ye need not one be left behind,
> For God hath bidden all mankind.
>
> Sent by my Lord, on you I call;
> The invitation is to all:
> Come, all the world; come, sinner, thou!
> All things in Christ are ready now.
>
> My message as from God receive,
> Ye all may come to Christ and live;
> O let His love your hearts constrain,
> Nor suffer Him to die in vain.

The amazing novelty of such a hymn and such an appeal is perhaps difficult to realise to-day, but to visualize that open-air scene is to see Methodism in the making.

RATTENBURY: *Wesley's Legacy to the World.*

THE RESULTING REFORMATION

Just at this time, when we wanted little of 'filling up the measure of our iniquities', two or three Clergymen of the Church of England began vehemently to 'call sinners to repentance'. In two or three years they had sounded the alarm to the utmost borders of the land. Many thousands gathered to hear them: and in every place where they came, many began to show such a concern for religion as they never had done before. A stronger impression was made on their minds, of the importance of things eternal, and they had more earnest desires of serving God than they had ever had from their earliest childhood. Thus did God begin to draw them toward himself, with the cords of love, with the bands of a man.

Many of these were in a short time deeply convinced of the number and heinousness of their sins. They were also made thoroughly sensible of those tempers which are justly hateful to God and man, and of their utter ignorance of God, and entire inability, either to know, love, or serve him. At the same time, they saw in the strongest light the insignificancy of their outside religion; nay, and often confessed it before God, as the most abominable hypocrisy. Thus did they sink deeper and deeper into that repentance which must ever precede faith in the Son of God.

And from hence sprung 'fruits meet for repentance'. The drunkard commenced sober and temperate; the whoremonger abstained from adultery and fornication; the unjust from oppression and wrong. He that had been accustomed to curse and swear for many years, now swore no more. The sluggard began to work with his hands, that he might eat his own bread. The miser learned to deal his bread to the hungry, and to cover the naked with a garment. Indeed, the whole form of their life was changed: They had left off doing evil, and learned to do well.

A Farther Appeal to Men of Reason and Religion.

Gospel Preaching: Its Results

On the other hand, when in my return I took an account of the Societies in Yorkshire, chiefly under the care of John Nelson, one of the *old* way, in whose preaching you could find no life, no food, I found them all alive, strong, and vigorous of soul, believing, loving, and praising God their Saviour, and increased in number from eighteen or nineteen hundred to upwards of three thousand. These had been continually fed with that wholesome food which *you* could neither relish nor digest. From the beginning they had been taught both the law and the gospel. 'God loves *you*: therefore love and obey *Him*. Christ died for *you*: therefore die to sin. Christ is risen: therefore rise in the image of God. Christ liveth evermore: therefore live to God, till you live with Him in glory.'

So *we* preached; and so *you* believed. This is the scriptural way, the *Methodist* way, the true way. God grant we may never turn therefrom, to the right hand or to the left.

Letter to Ebenezer Blackwell, December 20, 1751.

Chapter II

THE ETHICAL IDEAL: CHRISTIAN
PERFECTION OR PERFECT LOVE

WHAT ethical ideal did John Wesley uphold before his followers? By common consent, one of the most significant aspects
of the Revival was its call to Christian Perfection as the standard
of Christian living. The intention of the following quotations
is to indicate the importance of this, the main sources of Wesley's
teaching on the subject and the nature of Christian Perfection
as he conceived it. The final extract from the Sermon on Christian
Perfection is important as showing that Perfect Love is not free
from limits due to ignorance or errors of judgement, a very
sure and significant qualification. Even the saints may lack
knowledge and fail in judgement.

'In some ways the most important doctrine of all was Wesley's
doctrine of Christian Perfection, and important because its
emphasis was that the perfection of Christians was perfection
in love. . . . The doctrine was part of their great discovery
of God's universal love. For God's love shed abroad in our
hearts is a love that overflows in our love for our neighbour.
"We love because He first loved us." No perfection is possible
by a mere series of denials, however drastic. Perfection is to be
found in our affirmations and our actions, in the loving things
we do and say. Perfect Love, therefore, implies the social service
which some individualistic perfectionism has ignored. It is
love to God and love to our neighbour—and the love we feel
to God is not sincere, or at least it is undeveloped, unless it finds
its expression in love to others. The doctrine of perfect love
has been the most fruitful spring of action for Methodists.'

RATTENBURY: *Wesley's Legacy to the World* pp. 98–9.

WESLEY'S TEACHERS IN PERFECTION: JEREMY TAYLOR, THOMAS À KEMPIS, WILLIAM LAW AND THE BIBLE

In the year 1725, being in the twenty-third year of my
age, I met with Bishop Taylor's *Rule and Exercises of Holy
Living and Dying*. In reading several parts of this book, I was
exceedingly affected; that part in particular which relates
to purity of intention. Instantly I resolved to dedicate all
my life to God, all my thoughts, and words, and actions:

B   17

being thoroughly convinced, there was no medium; but that every part of my life (not some only) must either be a sacrifice to God, or myself, that is, in effect, to the devil.

Can any serious person doubt of this, or find a medium between serving God and serving the devil?

In the year 1726, I met with Kempis's *Christian Pattern*. The nature and extent of inward religion, the religion of the heart, now appeared to me in a stronger light than ever it had done before. I saw, that giving even all my life to God (supposing it possible to do this, and go no farther) would profit me nothing, unless I gave my heart, yea, all my heart, to him.

I saw, that 'simplicity of intention, and purity of affection', one design in all we speak or do, and one desire ruling all our tempers, are indeed 'the wings of the soul', without which she can never ascend to the mount of God.

A year or two after, Mr. Law's *Christian Perfection* and *Serious Call* were put into my hands. These convinced me, more than ever, of the absolute impossibility of being half a Christian; and I determined, through his grace (the absolute necessity of which I was deeply sensible of), to be all-devoted to God, to give him all my soul, my body, and my substance.

Will any considerate man say that this is carrying matters too far? or that anything less is due to him who has given himself for us, than to give him ourselves, all we have, and all we are?

In the year 1729, I began not only to read, but to study, the Bible, as the one, the only standard of truth, and the only model of pure religion. Hence I saw, in a clearer and clearer light, the indispensable necessity of having 'the mind which was in Christ', and of 'walking as Christ also walked'; even of having, not some part only, but all the mind which was in him; and of walking as he walked, not only in many or in most respects, but in all things. And this was the light, wherein at this time I generally considered religion, as a uniform following of Christ, an entire inward and outward conformity to our Master. Nor was I afraid of anything more, than of bending this rule to the experience of myself, or of other men; of allowing myself in any the least disconformity to our grand Exemplar.

WESLEY: *A Plain Account of Christian Perfection*.

CHRISTIAN PERFECTION

What is Christian Perfection? The loving God with all our heart, mind, soul and strength. This implies that no wrong temper, none contrary to love, remains in the soul; and that all the thoughts, words and actions are governed by pure love.

Conference of Preachers, 1759.

THE CHARACTER OF A METHODIST

What then is the mark? Who is a Methodist, according to your own account? I answer: A Methodist is one who has 'the love of God shed abroad in his heart by the Holy Ghost given unto him'; one who 'loves the Lord his God with all his heart, and with all his soul, and with all his mind, and with all his strength'. God is the joy of his heart, and the desire of his soul; which is constantly crying out, 'Whom have I in heaven but thee? and there is none upon earth that I desire beside thee! My God and my all! Thou art the strength of my heart, and my portion for ever!'

He is therefore happy in God, yea, always happy, as having in him 'a well of water springing up into everlasting life', and 'overflowing his soul with peace and joy'.

And while he thus always exercises his love to God, by praying without ceasing, rejoicing evermore, and in everything giving thanks, this commandment is written in his heart, 'That he who loveth God, love his brother also'. And he accordingly loves his neighbour as himself; he loves every man as his own soul. His heart is full of love to all mankind, to every child of 'the Father of the spirits of all flesh'. That a man is not personally known to him, is no bar to his love; no, nor that he is known to be such as he approves not, that he repays hatred for his good-will. For he 'loves his enemies'; yea, and the enemies of God, 'the evil and the unthankful'. And if it be not in his power to 'do good to them that hate him', yet he ceases not to pray for them, though they continue to spurn his love, and still 'despitefully use him and persecute him'.

For he is 'pure in heart'. The love of God has purified his heart from all revengeful passions, from envy, malice, and wrath, from every unkind temper or malign affection.

It hath cleansed him from pride and haughtiness of spirit, whereof alone cometh contention. And he hath now 'put on bowels of mercies, kindness, humbleness of mind, meekness, longsuffering': So that he 'forbears and forgives, if he had a quarrel against any; even as God in Christ hath forgiven him'.

All the commandments of God he accordingly keeps, and that with all his might. For his obedience is in proportion to his love, the source from whence it flows. And therefore, loving God with all his heart, he serves him with all his strength. He continually presents his soul and body a living sacrifice, holy, acceptable to God; entirely and without reserve devoting himself, all he has, and all he is, to his glory. All the talents he has received, he constantly employs according to his Master's will; every power and faculty of his soul, every member of his body. Once he 'yielded' them 'unto sin' and the devil, 'as instruments of unrighteousness'; but now, 'being alive from the dead, he yields' them all 'as instruments of righteousness unto God'.

By consequence, whatsoever he doeth, it is all to the glory of God. In all his employments of every kind, he not only aims at this (which is implied in having a single eye), but actually attains it. His business and refreshments, as well as his prayers, all serve this great end. Whether he sit in his house or walk by the way, whether he lie down or rise up, he is promoting, in all he speaks or does, the one business of his life, whether he put on his apparel, or labour, or eat and drink, or divert himself from too wasting labour, it all tends to advance the glory of God, by peace and goodwill among men. His one invariable rule is this, 'Whatsoever ye do, in word or deed, do it all in the name of the Lord Jesus, giving thanks to God and the Father by him'.

Nor do the customs of the world at all hinder his 'running the race that is set before him'. He knows that vice does not lose its nature, though it becomes ever so fashionable; and remembers, that 'every man is to give an account of himself to God'. He cannot, therefore, 'follow' even 'a multitude to do evil'. He cannot, 'fare sumptuously every day' or 'make provision for the flesh to fulfil the lusts thereof'. He cannot 'lay up treasures upon earth', any more than he can take fire into his bosom. He cannot 'adorn himself', on any pretence, 'with gold or costly apparel'. He cannot join in or countenance any diversion which has the least tendency to vice of any kind. He cannot 'speak evil' of his neighbour, any more than he can lie either for God or man. He cannot utter an unkind word of any one; for love keeps the door of his lips. He cannot speak 'idle words'; 'no corrupt communication' ever 'comes out of his mouth', as is all that 'which is' not 'good to the use of edifying' not 'fit to minister grace to the hearers'. But 'whatsoever things are pure, whatsoever things are lovely, whatsoever things are justly' of good report, 'he thinks, and speaks, and acts, adorning the gospel of our Lord Jesus Christ in all things'.

Lastly. As he has time, he 'does good unto all men'; unto neighbours and strangers, friends and enemies; and that in every possible kind; not only to their bodies, by 'feeding the hungry, clothing the naked, visiting those that are sick or in prison'; but much more does he labour to do good to their souls, as of the ability which God giveth; to awaken those that sleep in death; to bring those who are awakened to the atoning blood, that 'being justified by faith, they may have peace with God'; and to provoke those who have peace with God to abound more in love and in good works. And he is willing to 'spend and be spent herein', even 'to be offered up on the sacrifice and service of their faith', so they may 'all come unto the measure of the stature of the fulness of Christ'.

WESLEY: *The Character of a Methodist.*

THE LIMITS OF CHRISTIAN PERFECTION

No one, then, is so perfect in this life, as to be free from ignorance. Nor, secondly, from mistake; which is indeed almost an unavoidable consequence of it; seeing those who 'know but in part' are ever liable to err touching the things which they know not. It is true, the children of God do not mistake as to the things essential to salvation; they do not 'put darkness for light or light for darkness', neither 'seek death in the error of their life'. For they are 'taught of God'; and the way he teaches them, the way of holiness, is so plain, that 'the wayfaring man, though a fool, need not err therein'. But in things unessential to salvation they do err, and that frequently. The best and wisest of men are frequently mistaken even with regard to facts; believing those things not to have been which really were, or those to have been done which were not. Or, suppose they are not mistaken as to the fact itself, they may be with regard to its circumstances; believing them, or many of them, to have been quite different from what, in truth, they were. And hence cannot but arise many further mistakes. Hence they may believe either past or present actions which were or are evil, to be good; and such as were or are good, to be evil. Hence also they may judge not according to truth with regard to the characters of men; and that, not only by supposing good men to be better, or wicked men to be worse, than they are; but by believing them to have been or to be good men, who were or are very wicked; or perhaps those to have been or to be wicked men, who were or are holy and unreprovable.

Nay with regard to the holy Scriptures themselves, as careful as they are to avoid it, the best of men are liable to mistakes, and do mistake day by day; especially with respect to those parts thereof which less immediately relate to practice. Hence, even the children of God are not agreed as to the interpretation of many places in holy writ; nor is their difference of opinion any proof that they are not the children of God, on either side; but it is a proof that we are no more to expect any living man to be infallible, than to be omniscient.

WESLEY: *Sermon on Christian Perfection.*

CHAPTER III

THE CHRISTIAN AND THE USE OF MONEY

A PERTINENT illustration of the application of the rule of Christian Perfection was in regard to the acquisition and use of money. So important did Wesley conceive this to be that one of the Forty-Four *Standard Sermons* is devoted to it. The need that elicited the Sermon should be clearly recognized. One result of the Methodist Revival was the development of habits of industry, self-dependence, initiative and thrift. As a consequence, Methodists tended to become prosperous, whether as manufacturers, merchants or shopkeepers. This tendency called forth from Wesley continual warnings against the perils of wealth and insistence on the duties of philanthropy. In the *Journal* are references to sermons preached by Wesley in his later years on the danger of riches, and many comments occur in his letters about the growing wealth amongst members of the Society. The famous Forty-Fourth Sermon must be judged in the light of this almost 'medieval dread of riches'. The acquisition of wealth is not in itself felt to be wrong, and indeed is commended in so far as it is the result of honest industry. But the Sermon sets severe limits, both for self-regarding and other-regarding reasons, not only to the getting of money, but still more to its use, and in these limits, the other-regarding motives predominate over the self-regarding ones.

The Sermon, as a full account of the place and power of money in the social order, is not wholly satisfying to the Christian conscience of to-day. It assumes too readily individual effort as the basis of economic life, and it does not discern the possible need of social control over industry which succeeding generations were to recognize. But in its day and time, it served as a magnificent corrective to unrestrained greed of gain and un-disciplined use of wealth, and many a passage shows the Christian conscience sensitive and alert to the social responsibility attaching to the acquisition and use of wealth. In brief, the teaching of the Sermon is that love of our neighbour as ourself must govern the acquiring of money, that expenditure on luxury or worldly display is utterly to be deprecated in the Christian, and that when all reasonable needs of oneself and one's family are met, the chief value of money is to give it away in the service of God and man. Whatever criticism may be directed against the Sermon, there will be no doubt as to the ascetic discipline in work and spending which it demanded. The extracts from the Sermon are illustrated by one or two quotations from the *Journal* and the *Letters*.

A Warning Concerning Riches

I went on to Macclesfield, and found a people still alive to God, in spite of swiftly increasing riches. If they continue so, it will be the only instance I have known, in above half a century. I warned them in the strongest terms I could, and believe some of them had ears to hear.

Journal, March 31, 1787.

Out of Conceit with Those Who Have Riches

Most of those in England who have riches love money, even the Methodists, at least those who are called so. The poor are the Christians. I am quite out of conceit with almost all those who have this world's goods. Let us take care to lay up our treasure in heaven.

Letter to Freeborn Garrettson, November 30, 1786.

An Instance of Eighteenth-Century Luxury

In the afternoon we walked to Mr. Lascelles's house. It is finely situated on a little eminence, commanding a most delightful prospect, of hill and dale, and wood and water. It is built of a fine white stone, with two grand and beautiful fronts. I was not much struck with anything within. There is too much sameness in all the great houses I have seen in England; two rows of large, square rooms, with costly beds, glasses, chairs and tables. But here is a profusion of wealth; every pane of glass, we were informed, cost six and twenty shillings. One looking-glass cost five hundred pounds, and one bed, six hundred. The whole floor was just on the plan of Montague House, now the British Museum. The grounds round the house are pleasant indeed, particularly the walks on the riverside, and through the woods. But what has the owner thereof, save the beholding them with his eyes?

Journal, Friday, April 30, 1779.

On Money as an Instrument of Good

'The love of money', we know, 'is the root of all evil'; but not the thing itself. The fault does not lie in the money, but in them that use it. It may be used ill: and what may not? But it may likewise be used well: it is full as applicable to the best, as to the worst uses. It is of unspeakable service to all civilized nations, in all the common affairs of life: it is a most compendious instrument of transacting all manner of business, and (if we use it according to Christian wisdom) of doing all manner of good. It is true, were man in a state of innocence, or were all men 'filled with the Holy Ghost' so that, like the infant church at Jerusalem, 'no man counted anything he had his own', but 'distribution was made to every one as he had need', the use of it would be superseded; as we cannot conceive there is anything of the kind among the inhabitants of heaven. But, in the present state of mankind, it is an excellent gift of God, answering the noblest ends. In the hand of his children, it is food for the hungry, drink for the thirsty, raiment for the naked: it gives to the traveller and the stranger where to lay his head. By it we may supply the place of an husband to the widow, and of a father to the fatherless. We may be a defence for the oppressed, a means of health to the sick, of ease to them that are in pain; it may be as eyes to the blind, as feet to the lame; yea, a lifter up from the gates of death.

It is, therefore, of the highest concern, that all who fear God know how to employ this valuable talent; that they be instructed how it may answer these glorious ends, and in the highest degree. And, perhaps, all the instructions which are necessary for this may be reduced to three plain rules, by the exact observance whereof we may approve ourselves faithful stewards of 'the mammon of unrighteousness'.

WESLEY: *Sermon on the Use of Money*.

THE FIRST RULE: GAIN ALL YOU CAN! BUT——!

The first of these (rules) is 'Gain all you can'. Here we may speak like the children of the world: we meet them on their own ground. And it is our bounden duty to do this: we ought to gain all we can gain, without buying gold too dear, without paying more for it than it is worth. But this it is certain we ought not to do; we ought not to gain money at the expense of life, nor (which is in effect the same thing) at the expense of our health. Therefore, no gain whatsoever should induce us to enter into, or to continue in, any employ, which is of such a kind, or is attended with so hard or so long labour, as to impair our constitution. Neither should we begin or continue in any business which necessarily deprives us of proper seasons for food and sleep in such a proportion as our nature requires. Indeed, there is a great difference here. Some employments are absolutely and totally unhealthy; as those which imply the dealing much with arsenic, or other equally hurtful minerals, or the breathing an air tainted with streams of melting lead, which must at length destroy the firmest constitution.

We are, secondly, to gain all we can without hurting our mind any more than our body. For neither may we hurt this: we must preserve at all events, the spirit of a healthful mind. Therefore, we may not engage or continue in any sinful trade; any that is contrary to the law of God, or of our country. Such are all that necessarily imply our robbing or defrauding the king of his lawful customs. For it is, at least, as sinful to defraud the king of his right, as to rob our fellow subjects: and the king has full as much right to his customs as we have to our houses and apparel. Other businesses there are which, however innocent in themselves, cannot be followed with innocence now; at least not in England; such, for instance, as will not afford a competent maintenance without cheating or lying, or conformity to some custom which is not consistent with a good conscience: these, likewise, are sacredly to be avoided, whatever gain they may be attended with, provided we follow the custom of the trade; for, to gain money, we must not lose our souls.

We are, thirdly, to gain all we can, without hurting our neighbour. But this we may not, cannot do, if we love our neighbour as ourselves. We cannot, if we love every one as ourselves, hurt any one *in his substance*. We cannot devour the increase of his lands, and perhaps the lands and houses themselves, by *gaining*, by overgrown bills (whether on account of physic, or law, or anything else), or by requiring or taking such interest as even the laws of our country forbid. Hereby all pawnbroking is excluded: seeing, whatever good we might do thereby, all unprejudiced men see, with grief, to be abundantly overbalanced by the evil. And if it were otherwise, yet we are not allowed to 'do evil that good may come'. We cannot, consistent with brotherly love, sell our goods below the market price; we cannot study to ruin our neighbour's trade, in order to advance our own; much less can we entice away, or receive, any of his servants or work-men whom he has need of. None can gain by swallowing up his neighbour's substance, without gaining the damna-tion of hell! WESLEY: *Sermon on the Use of Money*.

HURT TO OUR NEIGHBOUR'S BODY: THE LIQUOR TRADE

Neither may we gain by hurting our neighbour *in his body*. Therefore we may not sell anything which tends to impair health. Such is, eminently, all the liquid fire, commonly called drams, or spirituous liquors. It is true, these may have a place in medicine; they may be of use in some bodily disorders; although there would rarely be occasion for them, were it not for the unskilfulness of the practitioner. Therefore, such as prepare and sell them only for this end may keep their conscience clear. But who are they? Who prepare them only for this end? Do you know ten such distillers in England? Then excuse these. But all who sell them in the common way, to any that will buy, are poisoners general. They murder His Majesty's subjects by wholesale, neither does their eye pity or spare. They drive them to hell, like sheep. And what is their gain? Is it not the blood of these men? Who then would envy their large estates and sumptuous palaces? A curse is in the midst of them: the curse of God cleaves to the stones, the timber, the furniture of them! The curse of God is in their gardens, their walks, their groves; a fire that burns to the nethermost hell! WESLEY: *Sermon on the Use of Money*.

HURT TO OUR NEIGHBOUR'S SOUL: THE PURVEYING OF SINFUL PLEASURE

This is dear-bought gain. And so is whatever is pro-cured by hurting our neighbour in his soul; by ministering, suppose, either directly or indirectly, to his unchastity or intemperance; which certainly none can do who has any fear of God, or any real desire of pleasing Him. It nearly concerns all those to consider this, who have any-thing to do with taverns, victualling-houses, opera-houses, play-houses, or any other places of public, fashionable diversion. If these profit the souls of men, you are clear;

your employment is good, and your gain innocent; but if they are either sinful in themselves, or natural inlets to sin of various kinds, then, it is to be feared, you have a sad account to make.

WESLEY: *Sermon on the Use of Money.*

SPARTAN LIVING: THE SECOND RULE: SAVE ALL YOU CAN!

Having gained all you can, by honest wisdom, and un-wearied diligence, the second rule of Christian prudence is, 'Save all you can'.

Waste no part of it in curiously adorning your houses; in superfluous or expensive furniture; in costly pictures, painting, gilding, books; in elegant rather than useful gardens.

Lay out nothing to gratify the pride of life, to gain the admiration or praise of men. This motive of expense is frequently interwoven with one or both of the former. Men are expensive in diet, or apparel or furniture, not barely to please their appetite, or to gratify their eye, or their imagination, but their vanity too.

Who would expend anything in gratifying these desires if he considered that to gratify them is to increase them? Nothing can be more certain than this: daily experience shows the more they are indulged, they increase the more.

WESLEY: *Sermon on the Use of Money.*

A QUESTION ABOUT INHERITANCE

'What then would you do, if you was in my case? if you had a considerable fortune to leave?' Whether I *would* do it or no I know what I *ought* to do: this will admit of no reasonable question. If I had one child, elder or younger, who knew the value of money, one who, I believed, would put it to the true use, I should think it my absolute, indispensable duty to leave that child the bulk of my fortune; and to the rest just so much as would enable them to live in the manner they had been accustomed to do. 'But what, if all your children were equally ignorant of the true use of money?' I ought then (hard saying! who can hear it?) to give each what would keep him above want; and to bestow all the rest in such a manner as I judged would be most for the glory of God.

WESLEY: *Sermon on the Use of Money.*

THE FINAL RULE: GIVE ALL YOU CAN!

All this is nothing if a man go not forward, if he does not point all this at a farther end. Nor indeed, can a man properly be said to save anything if he only lays it up. You may as well throw your money into the sea as bury it in the earth. And you may as well bury it in the the earth as in your chest, or in the Bank of England. Not to use, is effectually to throw it away. If, therefore, you would indeed 'make yourselves friends of the mammon of unrighteousness' add the third rule to the two preceding. Having, first, gained all you can, and, secondly, saved all you can, then 'give all you can'.

WESLEY: *Sermon on the Use of Money.*

DIVINE DIRECTIONS

The directions which God has given us, touching the use of our wordly substance, may be comprised in the following particulars. If you desire to be a faithful and a wise steward, out of that portion of your Lord's goods which he has for the present lodged in your hands, but with the right of resuming whenever it pleases him, first, provide things needful for yourself, food to eat, raiment to put on, whatever nature moderately requires for preserving the body in health and strength. Secondly, provide these for your wife, your children, your servants, or any others who pertain to your household. If, when this is done, there be an over-plus left, then 'do good to them that are of the household of faith'. If there be an over-plus still, 'as you have opportunity, do good unto all men'. In so doing you give all you can; nay, in a sound sense, all you have: for all that is laid out in this manner is really given to God. You 'render unto God the things that are God's', not only by what you give to the poor, but also by that which you expend in providing things needful for yourself and your household.

WESLEY: *Sermon on the Use of Money.*

CHRISTIAN PRUDENCE

You see the nature and extent of truly Christian prudence, so far as it relates to the use of that great talent, money. Gain all you can without hurting either yourself or your neighbour, in soul or body, by applying hereto with unintermitted diligence, and with all the understanding which God has given you;—save all you can, by cutting off every expense which serves only to indulge foolish desire; to gratify either the desire of the flesh, the desire of the eye, or the pride of life; waste nothing, living or dying, on sin or folly, whether for yourself or your children;—and then give all you can, or, in other words, give all you have to God.

WESLEY: *Sermon on the Use of Money.*

AN OXFORD METHODIST'S USE OF MONEY

One of them had thirty pounds a year. He lived on twenty-eight and gave away forty shillings. The next year, receiving sixty pounds, he still lived on twenty-eight, and gave away thirty-two. The third year he received ninety pounds, and gave away sixty-two. The fourth year he received a hundred and twenty pounds; still he lived as before on twenty-eight, and gave to the poor all the rest.

WESLEY (*speaking of himself as a Fellow of Lincoln*), quoted in '*New History of Methodism*', p. 142.

'MONEY NEVER STAYS WITH ME'

Dear Patty,

You do not consider, money never stays with *me* ; it would burn me if it did. I throw it out of my hands as soon as possible, lest it should find a way into my heart. Therefore you should have spoken to me while I was in London, and before Miss Lewen's money flew away. However, I know not but I may still spare you five pounds, provided you will not say, 'I will never ask you again', because that is more than you can tell; and you must not promise more than you can perform.   *Letter to Mrs. Hall, Oct.* 6, 1768.

PLAIN WORDS TO A MAN OF WEALTH.

SIR,

Whether I see you any more in this life, or no, I rejoice that I have seen you this once, and that God enabled you to bear with patience what I spoke in the simplicity of my heart.

The substance of what I took the liberty to mention to you this morning was: You are on the borders of the grave, as well as I; shortly we must both appear before God. When it seemed to me, some months since, that my life was near an end, I was troubled that I had not dealt plainly with you. This you will permit me to do now, without any reserve, in the fear and in the presence of God.

I reverence you for your office as a magistrate; I believe you to be an honest, upright man; I love you for having protected an innocent people from their cruel and lawless oppressors. But so much the more am I obliged to say (though I judge not; God is the judge), I fear you are covetous, that you love the world. And if you do, as sure as the Word of God is true, you are not in a state of salvation.

The substance of your answer was: That many people exhort others to charity from self-interest; that men of fortune must mind their fortune; that you cannot go about to look for poor people; that when you have seen them yourself, and relieved them, they were scarce ever satisfied; that many make an ill use of what you give them; that you cannot trust the account people give of themselves by letters; that nevertheless you do give to private persons by the hands of Colonel Hudson and others; that you have also given to several hospitals an hundred pounds at a time, but that you must support your family; that the Lowther family has continued above four hundred years; that you are for great things—for public charities, and for saving the nation from ruin; and that others may think as they please, but this is your way of thinking, and has been for many years.

To this I replied (1) Sir, I have no self-interest in this matter; I consult your interest, not my own; I want nothing from you, I desire nothing from you, I expect nothing from you. But I am concerned for your immortal spirit, which must so soon launch into eternity. (2) It is true men of fortune must mind their fortune; but they must not love the world. 'If any man love the world, the love of the Father is not in him.' (3) It is true likewise you cannot go about to look for poor people; but you may be sufficiently informed of them by those that can. (4) And if some of these are never satisfied, this is no reason for not relieving others. (5) Suppose, too, that some make an ill use of what you give, the loss falls on their own head. You will not lose your reward for their fault. What you laid out, God will pay you again. (6) Yet certainly you do well to have all the assurance you can that those to whom you give are likely to make a good use of it; and therefore to expect a stronger recommendation of them than their own, whether by letter or otherwise. (7) I rejoice that you have given to many by so worthy a man as Colonel Hudson, whose word is certainly a sufficient recommendation. (8) I rejoice likewise that you have given some hundreds of pounds to the hospitals, and wish it had been ten thousand. (9) To the support of the family I did not object; but begged leave to ask, whether this could not be done without giving ten thousand a year to one who had as much already? and whether you could answer this to God in the day wherein he shall judge the world? (10) I likewise granted that the family had continued above four hundred years; but observed meantime that God regarded it not one jot the more for this, and that four hundred or one thousand years are but a moment compared to eternity. (11) I observed likewise that great things may be done and little things not left undone. (12) And that if this or any other way of thinking be according to Scripture, then it is sound and good; whereas, if it be contrary to Scripture, it is not good, and the longer we are in it so much the worse.

Upon the whole, I must once more earnestly entreat you to consider yourself and God and eternity. (1) As to yourself, you are not the proprietor of anything—no, not of one shilling in the world. You are only a steward of what another entrusts you with, to be laid out not according to your will but his. And what would you think of your steward if he laid out what is called your money according to his own will and pleasure? (2) Is not God the sole proprietor of all things? And are you not to give an account to him for every part of his goods? And oh how dreadful an account, if you have expended any part of them not according to his will but your own! (3) Is not death at hand? And are not you and I just stepping into eternity? Are we not just going to appear in the presence of God, and that naked of all worldly goods? Will you then rejoice in the money you have left behind you? or in that you have given to support a family, as it is called—that is, in truth, to support the pride and vanity and luxury which you have yourself despised all your life long? O, sir, I beseech you, for the sake of God, for the sake of your own immortal soul, examine yourself whether you do not love money. If so, you cannot love God. And if we die without the fear of God, what remains? Only to be banished from him for ever and ever!

I am, with true respect, sir,

Your servant for Christ's sake.

Letter to Sir James Lowther, October 28, 1754.

THE DANGERS OF PROSPERITY

The dangers of prosperity are great; and you seem aware of them. If poverty contracts and depresses the mind, riches sap its fortitude, destroy its vigour, and nourish its caprices.

Letter to Dr. Wrangel, January 30, 1770.

CONCERNING SILVER PLATE

Bristol, September 9, 1776.

SIR,

I have two silver tea-spoons at London and two at Bristol. This is all the plate which I have at present. And I shall not buy any more while so many round me want bread.

I am, Sir,

Your most humble servant.

Letter to the Commissioner of Excise (in reply to a special letter requiring an immediate answer, intimating that it could not be doubted he had plate. The House of Lords had ordered circular letters should be sent to all persons possessing silver plate, but having made no return of it or failed to pay duty).

A LIFE-LONG HABIT

For upwards of eighty-six years I have kept my accounts exactly. I will not attempt it any longer, being satisfied with the continual conviction that I save all I can, and give all I can—that is, all I have.

WESLEY: *Last Entry in His Personal Account Book, 1790.*

c

CHAPTER IV

THE PRACTICE OF PHILANTHROPY, PRIVATE AND PUBLIC

WESLEY'S answer to the problem of the unequal distribution of wealth and the existence of social need was a wide-flung and persistent personal philanthropy. This was rooted in a deep concern for the poor and destitute, felt even in his Oxford days and quickened by his Evangelical faith and experience. Thus did his burning love for men find one avenue of expression. His hatred of luxury was associated with his sense of the need of the poor, to which the extravagances of the rich stood in such utter contrast. With the one he was impatient; over the other his heart yearned.

Eighteenth-century poverty bore the general marks of destitution in any age, but it had its own particular origins and characteristics. Low wages in agriculture and amongst miners and the new industrialists beginning to flock into the towns were one cause. The recurrent wars in which England was engaged during the century produced their inevitable aftermath in increased national debt, taxation and declining trade with consequent unemployment. Poor harvests from time to time added to the general distress. Wesley's pamphlet, *Thoughts on the Present Scarcity of Provisions*, dated 1773, comes at the end of the first decade after the Seven Years' War. It is clear, however, that there was a general lack of concern for the poor among the possessing classes, with which Wesley was continually at war, and which made him press so insistently the Christian duty of caring for our neighbour and relieving the needs of the poor. What is more, he followed his precepts with action, and there are few more moving entries in his *Journal* than those in which he describes some new movement of his philanthropy.

Did Wesley ever envisage more than the practice of private philanthropy as a redress for existing social injustice? What would have been his attitude to social legislation directed to this end, such as has become so common in our time in every advanced nation? Any answer must be speculative. On the one side, his political proclivities would be likely to make him resist changes in the constitution which would involve radical alteration in social structure. Yet, on the other hand, in the pamphlet already referred to, *Thoughts on the Present Scarcity of Pro-*

visions, he puts forward legislative proposals directed to the alleviation of the existing burden of poverty. Whatever we may think of the enactments he proposes, prohibit distilling, reduce taxation, abolish useless pensions, discharge half the National Debt—the fact that he can put them forward at all is significant. It suggests that if he had lived in a later age, the depth of his concern for the poor would have carried him further along the line of social legislation, if he had become convinced that social justice demanded it, and that he would have pressed on any government the duty and obligation of enacting it. As it is, we discover him projecting schemes of social betterment from homes for orphans and widows to medical dispensaries, strangers' benevolent societies and loan clubs, in the evident conviction that these were practical objects to be undertaken by the Christian community in fulfilment of the obligation of perfect love. In what a practical spirit these were conceived the single example of his loan club may be cited. Wesley had conceived a great antipathy to pawnbrokers, by reason of the exorbitant interest charged. His loan club was a Christian alternative.

THE CONDITION OF THE POOR

I ask, first, why are thousands of people starving, perishing for want, in every part of the nation? The fact I know ; I have seen it with my eyes, in every corner of the land. I have known those who could only afford to eat a little coarse food once every other day. I have known one in London (and one that a few years before had all the conveniences of life) picking up from a dunghill stinking sprats and carrying them home for herself and her children. I have known another gathering the bones which the dogs had left in the streets, and making broth of them, to prolong a wretched life! I have heard a third artlessly declare, 'Indeed I was very faint, and so weak I could hardly walk, until my dog, finding nothing at home, went out, and brought in a good sort of bone, which I took out of his mouth, and made a pure dinner!' Such is the case at this day of multitudes of people, in a land flowing, as it were, with milk and honey! abounding with all the necessaries, the conveniences, the superfluities of life!

Now, why is this? Why have all these nothing to eat? Because they have nothing to do. The plain reason why they have no meat is because they have no work.

But why have they no work? Why are so many thousand

people, in London, in Bristol, in Norwich, in every county, from one end of England to the other, utterly destitute of employment?

Because the persons that used to employ them cannot afford to do it any longer. Many that employed fifty men, now scarce employ ten; those that employed twenty, now employ one, or none at all. They cannot, as they have no vent for their goods; food being so dear, that the generality of people are hardly able to buy anything else.

WESLEY: *Thoughts on the Present Scarcity of Provisions*, 1773.

WESLEY'S LOVE OF THE POOR

. . . . In most genteel religious people there is so strange a mixture that I have seldom much confidence in them. I love the poor; in many of them I find pure, genuine grace, unmixed with paint, folly, and affectation.

Letter to Dorothy Furly, September 25, 1757.

I have found some of the uneducated poor who have exquisite taste and sentiment; and many, very many, of the rich who have scarcely any at all. But I do not speak of this; I want you to converse more, abundantly more, with the poorest of the people, who, if they have not any taste, have souls, which you may forward in their way to heaven. And they have (many of them) faith and the love of God in a larger measure than any persons I know. Creep in among these in spite of dirt and an hundred disgusting circumstances, and thus put off the gentlewoman. Do not confine your conversation to genteel and elegant people. I should like this as well as you do; but I cannot discover a precedent for it in the life of our Lord or any of His Apostles. My dear friend, let you and I walk as He walked.

Letter to Miss March, February 7, 1776.

AT OXFORD

Upon this encouragement we still continued to meet together as usual; and to confirm one another, as well as we could, in our resolutions, to communicate as often as we had opportunity (which is here once a week), and do what service we could to our acquaintance, the prisoners, and two or three poor families in the town. But the outcry daily increasing, that we might show what ground there was for it, we proposed to our friends, or opponents, as we had opportunity, these, or the like questions:—

Whether it does not concern all men of all conditions to imitate Him, as much as they can, 'who went about doing good'?

Whether all Christians are not concerned in that command, 'While we have time let us do good to all men'?

Whether we can be happy at all hereafter, unless we have, according to our power, 'fed the hungry, clothed the naked, visited those that are sick, and in prison', and made all these actions subservient to a higher purpose, even the saving of souls from death?

Whether it be not our bounden duty always to remember, that He did more for us than we can do for Him, who assures us, 'Inasmuch as ye have done it unto one of the least of these my brethren, ye have done it unto me'?

Whether, upon the considerations above-mentioned, we may not try to do good to those that are hungry, naked, or sick? In particular, whether, if we know any necessitous family, we may not give them a little food, clothes, or physic, as they want?

Whether we may not contribute, what little we are able, toward having their children clothed and taught to read?

Lastly, whether, upon the considerations above mentioned, we may not try to do good to those that are in prison? In particular, whether we may not release such well-disposed persons as remain in prison for small sums?

Whether we may not lend smaller sums to those that are of any trade, that they may procure themselves tools and materials to work with?

Whether we may not give to them who appear to want it most, a little money, or clothes, or physic?

Whether we may not supply as many as are serious enough to read, with a Bible, and *Whole Duty of Man?*

Letter to Mr. Morgan, senior, quoted in Preface to the Journal.

VISITING THE SICK

It was not long before the Stewards found a great difficulty with regard to the sick. Some were ready to perish before they knew of their illness; and when they did know, it was not in their power (being persons generally employed in trade) to visit them so often as they desired.

When I was apprized of this, I laid the case at large before the whole society; showed how impossible it was for the Stewards to attend all that were sick in all parts of the town; desired the Leaders of classes would more carefully inquire, and more constantly inform them, who were sick; and asked, 'Who among you is willing, as well as able, to supply this lack of service?'

The next morning many willingly offered themselves. I chose six-and-forty of them, whom I judged to be of the most tender, loving spirit; divided the town into twenty-three parts, and desired two of them to visit the sick in each division.   WESLEY: *The People called Methodists*, 1748.

STARTS A DISPENSARY

I was still in pain for many of the poor that were sick; there was so great expense, and so little profit. And first, I resolved to try, whether they might not receive more benefit in the hospitals. Upon the trial, we found there was indeed less expense, but no more good done, than before. I then asked the advice of several physicians for them; but still it profited not. I saw the poor people pining away, and several families ruined, and that without remedy.

At length I thought of a kind of desperate expedient. 'I will prepare, and give them physic myself.' For six or seven and twenty years, I had made anatomy and physic the diversion of my leisure hours; though I never properly studied them, unless for a few months when I was going to America, where I imagined I might be of some service to those who had no regular physician among them. I applied to it again. I took into my assistance an Apothecary, and an experienced Surgeon; resolving, at the same time, not to go out of my depth, but to leave all difficult and complicated cases to such physicians as the patients should choose.

I gave notice of this to the society; telling them, that all who were ill of chronical distempers (for I did not care to venture upon acute) might, if they pleased, come to me at such a time, and I would give them the best advice I could, and the best medicines I had.

Many came. In five months, medicines were occasionally given to above five hundred persons. Several of these I never saw before; for I did not regard whether they were of the society or not. In that time seventy-one of these, regularly taking their medicines, and following the regimen prescribed (which three in four would not do) were entirely cured of distempers long thought to be incurable. The whole expense of medicines during this time, was nearly forty pounds. We continued this ever since, and, by the blessing of God, with more and more success.   WESLEY: *The People called Methodists.*

A HOME FOR WIDOWS

I had for some years observed many who, although not sick, were not able to provide for themselves, and had none who took care to provide for them: These were chiefly feeble, aged widows. I consulted with the Stewards, how they might be relieved. They all agreed, if we could keep them in one house, it would not only be far less expensive to us, but also far more comfortable for them. Indeed we had no money to begin; but we believed He would provide, 'who defendeth the cause of the widow'. So we took a lease of two little houses near; we fitted them up, so as to be warm and clean. We took in as many widows as we had room for, and provided them with things needful for the body; toward the expense of which I set aside, first, the weekly contributions of the bands, and then all that was collected at the Lord's Supper. It is true, this does not suffice: So that we are considerably in debt, on this account also. But we are persuaded, it will not always be so; seeing 'the earth is the Lord's, and the fulness thereof'.

In this (commonly called The Poor House) we have now nine widows, one blind woman, two poor children, two upper-servants, a maid and a man. I might add, four or five preachers; for I myself, as well as the other preachers who are in town, diet with the poor, on the same food, and at the same table; and we rejoice herein, as a comfortable earnest of our eating bread together in our Father's kingdom.   WESLEY: *The People called Methodists*.

A School for Poor Children

Another thing which had given me frequent concern was, the case of abundance of children. Some their parents could not afford to put to school: So they remained like 'a wild ass's colt'. Others were sent to school, and learned, at least, to read and write; but they learned all kind of vice at the same time: So that it had been better for them to have been without their knowledge, than to have bought it at so dear a price.

At length I determined to have them taught in my own house, that they might have an opportunity of learning to read, write, and cast accounts (if no more), without being under almost a necessity of learning Heathenism at the same time: And after several unsuccessful trials, I found two such schoolmasters as I wanted; men of honesty and of sufficient knowledge, who had talents for, and their hearts in, the work.

They have now under their care nearly sixty children: The parents of some pay for their schooling; but the greater part, being very poor, do not; so that the expense is chiefly defrayed by voluntary contributions. We have of late clothed them too, as many as wanted.

WESLEY: *The People called Methodists*.

A Loan Society

A year or two ago, I observed among many a distress of another kind. They frequently wanted, perhaps in order to carry on their business, a present supply of money. They scrupled to make use of a pawnbroker; but where to borrow it they knew not. I resolved to try if we could not find a remedy for this also. I went, in a few days, from one end of the town to the other, and exhorted those who had this world's goods, to assist their needy brethren. Fifty pounds were contributed. This was immediately lodged in the hands of two Stewards; who attended every Tuesday morning, in order to lend to those who wanted any small sum, not exceeding twenty shillings, to be repaid within three months.

It is almost incredible, but it manifestly appears from their accounts, that, with this inconsiderable sum, two hundred and fifty have been assisted, within the space of one year. Will not God put it into the heart of some lover of mankind to increase this little stock? If this is not 'lending unto the Lord', what is?

WESLEY: *The People called Methodists.*

'IF THINE ENEMY HUNGER, FEED HIM'

I walked up to Knowle, a mile from Bristol, to see the French prisoners. Above eleven hundred of them, we were informed, were confined in that little place without anything to lie on but a little dirty straw, or anything to cover them but a few foul, thin rags, either by day or night, so that they died like rotten sheep. I was much affected, and preached in the evening on Exod. xxiii. 9: 'Thou shalt not oppress a stranger; for ye know the heart of a stranger, seeing ye were strangers in the land of Egypt.' Eighteen pounds were contributed immediately, which were made up four-and-twenty the next day. With this we bought linen and woollen cloth, which were made up into shirts, waistcoats, and breeches; some dozen of stockings were added: all which were carefully distributed where there was the greatest want. Presently after, the Corporation of Bristol sent a large quantity of mattresses and blankets; and it was not long before contributions were set on foot at London, and in various parts of the kingdom, so that I believe from this time they were pretty well provided with all the necessaries of life. *Journal, Monday, October* 15, 1759.

LETTER TO THE PRESS ABOUT PRISONERS OF WAR

SIR,

Since I came to Bristol I heard many terrible accounts concerning the French prisoners at Knowle—as that 'they were so wedged together that they had no room to breathe'; that 'the stench of the rooms where they lodged was intolerable'; that 'their food was only fit for dogs'; that 'their meat was carrion, their bread rotten and unwholesome'; and that, 'in consequence of this inhuman treatment, they died in whole shoals'.

Desiring to know the truth, I went to Knowle on Monday,

and was showed all the apartments there. But how was I disappointed! (1) I found they had large and convenient space to walk in, if they chose it, all the day. (2) There was no stench in any apartment which I was in, either below or above. They were all sweeter and cleaner than any prison I have seen either in England or elsewhere. (3) Being permitted to go into the larder, I observed the meat hanging up, two large quarters of beef. It was fresh and fat, and I verily think as good as I ever desire to eat. (4) A large quantity of bread lay on one side. A gentleman took up and cut one of the loaves. It was made of good flour, was well-baked, and perfectly well-tasted. (5) Going thence to the hospital I found that even in this sickly season there are not thirty persons dangerously ill out of twelve or thirteen hundred. (6) The hospital was sweeter and cleaner throughout than any hospital I ever saw in London. I think it my duty to declare these things, for clearing the innocent and the honour of the English nation.

Yet one thing I observed with concern. A great part of these men are almost naked; and winter is now coming upon them in a cold prison and a colder climate than most of them have been accustomed to. But will not the humanity and generosity of the gentlemen of Bristol prevent or relieve this distress? Did they not make a notable precedent during the late war? And surely they are not weary of well-doing. Tuesday night *we* did a little according to our power; but I shall rejoice if this beforgotten through the abundance administered by their liberality in a manner which they judge most proper. Will it not be both for the honour of their city and country, for the credit of our religion, and for the glory of God, who knows how to return it sevenfold into their bosom?

> I am,
> Your humble servant.

Letter to Editor of 'Lloyd's Evening Post', October 20, 1759.

I WAS IN PRISON, AND YE VISITED ME!

SIR,

On Sunday, December 16th last, I received a £20 Bank bill from an anonymous correspondent, who desired me to lay it out in the manner I judged best for the use of poor prisoners. I immediately employed some in whom I could confide to inquire into the circumstances of those confined in Whitechapel and New Prison. I knew the former to have very little allowance even of bread, and the latter none at all. Upon inquiry they found one poor woman in Whitechapel Prison very big with child and destitute of all things. At the same time I casually heard of a poor man who had been confined for nine months in the Poultry Compter, while his wife and three children (whom he before maintained by his labour) were almost perishing through want. Not long after, another poor woman, who had been diligent in helping others, was herself thrown into Whitechapel Prison. The expense of discharging these three and giving them a few necessaries amounted to £10 10s. 0d. One pound fourteen shillings I expended in stockings and other clothing, which was given to those prisoners who were in the most pressing want. The remainder, £7 16s. was laid out in bread, which was warily distributed thrice a week. I am therefore assured that the whole of this sum was laid out in real charity. And how much more noble a satisfaction must result from this to the generous benefactor (even supposing there were no other world, supposing man to die as a beast dieth) than he could receive from an embroidered suit of clothes or a piece of plate made in the newest fashion! Men of reason, judge!

      I am, sir,
          Your humble servant.

Letter to Editor of 'Lloyd's Evening Post,' February 18, 1760.

SIR,

Of all the seats of woe on this side of hell few, I suppose, exceed or even equal Newgate. If any region of horror could exceed it a few years ago, Newgate in Bristol did; so great was the filth, the stench, the misery, and wickedness which shocked all who had a spark of humanity left. How was I surprised, then, when I was there a few weeks ago! (1) Every part of it, above stairs and below, even *the pit* wherein the felons are confined at night, is as clean and sweet as a gentleman's house; it being now a rule that every prisoner wash and clean his apartment thoroughly twice a week. (2) Here is no fighting or brawling. If any thinks himself ill-used, the cause is immediately referred to the Keeper, who hears the contending parties face to face and decides the affair at onc . (3) The usual grounds of quarrelling are removed; for it is very rarely that any one cheats or wrongs another, as being sure, if anything of this kind is discovered, to be committed to a closer confinement. (4) Here is no drunkenness suffered, however advantageous it might be to the Keeper as well as the tapster. (5) Nor any whoredom, the women prisoners being narrowly observed and kept separate from the men; nor is any women of the town now admitted—no, not at any price. (6) All possible care is taken to prevent idleness; those who are willing to work at their callings are provided with tools and materials, partly by the Keeper, who gives them credit at a very moderate profit; partly by the alms occasionally given, which are divided with the utmost prudence and impartiality. Accordingly at this time, among others, a shoe-maker, a tailor, a brazier, and a coachmaker are working at their several trades. (7) Only on the Lord's Day they neither work nor play, but dress themselves as clean as they can, to attend the public service in the chapel, at which every person under the roof is present. None is excused unless sick; in which case he is provided gratis both with advice and medicines. (8) And, in order to assist them in things of the greatest concern (besides a sermon every Sunday and Thursday), they have a large Bible chained on one side of the chapel, which any of the prisoners may read. By the blessing of God on these regulations the prison now has a new face: nothing offends either the eye or ear; and the whole has the appearance of a quiet, serious family. And does not the Keeper of Newgate deserve to be remembered full as well as *the Man of Ross*? May the Lord Remember him in that day! Meantime will not one follow his example?

I am, sir,

Your humble servant.

Letter to the Editor of the 'London Chronicle', January 2, 1761.

BEFRIENDING THE STRANGER

REVEREND AND DEAR SIR,

A few of us are subscribing a penny a week each, which is to be carried on the Sabbath by one of ourselves, who read and pray with the afflicted, who, according to the rules enclosed, must be poor strangers, having no parish, or friend at hand to help them. Our benevolent plan is opposed by my class-leader; therefore we are constrained to seek your approbation before we proceed. We are very poor, and our whole stock is not yet twenty-shillings: will thank you, therefore, for any assistance you may please to afford your very humble servant,—JOHN GARDNER.

Letter from John Gardner to John Wesley.

MY DEAR BROTHER, December 31st, 1785.

I like the design and rules of your little Society and hope you will do good to many. I will subscribe threepence per week, and will give you a guinea in advance if you call on me Saturday morning.

I am,

Your affectionate brother,

JOHN WESLEY.

Wesley's reply, from which dates the Stranger's Friend Society, still existing in Liverpool and Bristol. Gardner became a doctor, and is buried in St. Leonard's, Shoreditch, with the curious epitaph, 'Dr. John Gardner, Last and best Bedroom', 1807.

DISTRIBUTING TO THE NECESSITIES OF SAINTS

DEAR SIR,

The money you left in my hands was disposed of as follows:—

	£	s.	d.
To the Lending Stock, ...	2	2	0
To Eliz. Brooks, expecting daily to have her goods seized for rent	1	1	0
To Eliz. Room (a poor widow) for rent, . .	0	5	0
Toward clothing Mary Middleton and another poor woman almost naked, . .	0	10	0
To John Edgar, a poor weaver, out of work .	0	5	0
To Lucy Jones, a poor orphan . .	0	2	0
To a poor family, for food and fuel, .	0	5	0
To Christopher Brown, out of business .	0	2	6
To an ancient woman in great distress .	0	2	6
Distributed among several sick families, .	0	10	0
	5	5	0

I am dear Sir, your affectionate servant.

Letter to Ebenezer Blackwell, February 4, 1751.

Observing the deep poverty of many of our brethren, I determined to do what I could for their relief. I spoke severally to some that were in good circumstances, and received about forty pounds. Next I inquired, Who were in the most pressing want, and visited them at their own houses. I was surprised to find no murmuring spirits among them, but many that were truly happy in God; and all of them appeared to be exceeding thankful for the scanty relief which they received.

Journal, Bristol, Friday, September 26, 1783. (*Wesley is* 80.)

All my leisure hours this week I employed in visiting the remaining poor, and in begging for them. Having collected about fifty pounds more, I was enabled to relieve most of those that were in pressing distress.

Journal, Bath, Wednesday, October 1, 1783.

At this season we usually distribute coals and bread among the poor of the Society; but I now considered they wanted clothes as well as food; so on this and the four following days I walked through the town, and begged two hundred pounds, in order to clothe them that wanted it most; but it was hard work, as most of the streets were filled with melting snow, which often lay ankle deep, so that my feet were steeped in snow-water nearly from morning till evening. I held it out pretty well till Saturday evening, when I was laid up with a violent flux, which increased every hour, till at six in the morning, Dr. Whitehead called upon me. His first draught made me quite easy, and three or four more perfected the cure.

Journal, London, Tuesday, January 4, 1785. (*At age of* 82.)

Monday the 8th, and the four following days, I went a-begging for the poor. I hoped to be able to provide food and raiment for those of the Society who were in pressing want, yet had no weekly allowance. These were about two hundred. But I was much disappointed. Six or seven indeed of our brethren gave ten pounds a-piece. If forty or fifty had done this, I could have carried my design into execution. However, much good was done with two hundred pounds, and many sorrowful hearts made glad.

Journal, Monday, January 8, 1787.

POVERTY, A SOCIAL EVIL: WHAT SHOULD GOVERNMENT DO?

What remedy is there for this sore evil, many thousand poor people are starving? Find them work, and you will find them meat. They will then earn and eat their own bread.

But how can the masters give them work without ruining themselves? Procure vent for what is wrought, and the masters will give them as much work as they can do. And this would be done by sinking the price of provisions; for then people would have money to buy other things too.

But how can the price of wheat and barley be reduced? By prohibiting for ever, by making a full end of that bane of health, that destroyer of strength, of life and of virtue— distilling. Perhaps this alone might go a great way toward answering the whole design. It is not improbable, it would speedily sink the price of corn, at least one part in three. If anything more were required, might not all starch be made of rice, and the importation of this, as well as of corn, be encouraged?

How can the price of oats be reduced? By reducing the number of horses. And may not this be effectually done (without affecting the ploughman, the waggoner, or any of those who keep horses for common work) (1) By laying a tax of ten pounds on every horse exported to France, for which (notwithstanding an artful paragraph in a late public paper) there is as great a demand as ever? (2) By laying an additional tax on gentlemen's carriages? Not so much on every wheel (barefaced, shameless partiality!), but five pounds yearly upon every horse. And would not these two taxes alone supply near as much as is now paid for leave to poison His Majesty's liege subjects?

How can the price of beef and mutton be reduced? By increasing the breed of sheep and horned cattle. And this would soon be increased sevenfold, if the price of horses was reduced; which it surely would be, half in half, by the method above mentioned.

How can the price of pork and poultry be reduced? Whether it ever will, is another question. But it can be done, (1) By letting no farms of above an hundred pounds a year: (2) By repressing luxury; whether by laws, by example, or by both. I had almost said, by the grace of God; but to mention this has been long out of fashion.

How may the price of land be reduced? By all the methods above-named, as each tends to lessen the expense of housekeeping: But especially the last; by restraining luxury, which is the grand and general source of want.

How may the taxes be reduced? (1) By discharging half the national debt, and so saving, by this single means, above two millions a year. (2) By abolishing all useless pensions, as fast as those who now enjoy them die: Especially those ridiculous ones given to some hundreds of idle men, as Governors of forts or castles; which forts have answered no end for above these hundred years, unless to shelter jackdaws and crows. Might not good part of a million more be saved in this very article?

But will this ever be done? I fear not: At least, we have no reason to hope for it shortly; for what good can we expect (suppose the Scriptures are true) for such a nation as this, where there is no fear of God, where there is such a deep, avowed, thorough contempt of all religion, as I never saw, never heard or read of, in any other nation, whether Christian, Mahometan, or Pagan? It seems as if God must shortly arise and maintain his own cause. But, if so, let us fall into the hands of God, and not into the hands of men.

Thoughts on the Present Scarcity of Provisions, 1773.

CHAPTER V

CONTEMPORARY SOCIAL HABITS

THE low standard of social life in eighteenth-century England, following on the dissolution of morals after the Restoration, is a frequent theme of historians of the period. Lecky, for example, reflects on the evil consequences of spirit drinking when men could get drunk for one penny and dead drunk for two-pence. Gambling seems to have had an equal hold on the people. Public lotteries were in vogue; at Brookes', the famous Club hard by St. James's Palace, fortunes were lost and won every night, and Hogarth's cartoons show men wagering in cockpits and street arabs playing with dice for money. Despite the existence of appalling poverty, it was an easy-going, luxurious, pleasure-loving age.

How did Wesley re-act to these things? It is undoubted that the revival he promoted brought a reformation of manners and a new sobriety and discipline of life. Luxury he reprobated, drunkenness, buying or selling spirituous liquors, or drinking them (unless in cases of extreme necessity), were not permitted to members of the Methodist Societies; nor, according to one of his letters, was addiction to gambling. But his judgement on these things was evidently determined by the hindrance they offered to the cause of religion and the harm they did to men's souls. The first evil in English life he deplores is godlessness.

This is the insistent note of his *Appeal to Men of Reason* published in 1745, and reiterated over and over again until his *Estimate of the Manners of the Present Times* in 1782, when he roundly declares that not sloth and luxury, though they exist, are the present characteristics of the English nation as distinct from other nations, but ungodliness. This continued to alarm him to the very end, the more so that in *A Serious Address to the People of England, with regard to the State of the Nation* in 1778, he is able to rebut the argument of those who at that time were loudly proclaiming the downpath of national prosperity by pointing out that actually England was in a far better state than it had been eighteen years previously, and even bordering on eminent prosperity.

In this section, therefore, we bring together some of his reflections on the godlessness and profanity of English life as he saw it, and, consequent upon this, indications of his attitude to luxury, insobriety and gambling. On these it must be added that while his repudiation of the first two is clear and unmistakable, some degree of ambiguity attaches to his attitude to gambling. His allusions to it are less frequent and vehement, and he apparently does not condemn public lotteries. On the other hand, his scornful allusion to a 'gaming Churchman' points to a clear recognition of the incongruity of the combination, the extravagances of the gaming table obviously came under the condemnation of a profligate use of money, and in one important letter he emphatically states that neither dancing nor playing at cards are permitted to members of the Methodist Societies. The letter is instructive also because it shows Wesley's sanity of temper in dealing with '*those that are without*', that is, people of the world, in regard to such amusements.

The Condition of England: Sloth and Luxury

Some years ago an ingenious man published a treatise with this title. According to him, the characteristics of the English at present are sloth and luxury. And thus much we may allow, that neither the one nor the other ever abounded in England as they do at this day. With regard to sloth, it was the constant custom of our ancestors to rise at four in the morning. This was the stated hour, summer and winter, for all that were in health. The two Houses of Parliament met 'at five'; *hora quinta antemeridiana*, says their *Journal*. But how is it with people of fashion now? They can hardly huddle on their clothes before eight or nine o'clock in the morning; perhaps some of them not before twelve. And when they are risen, what do they do?

> They waste away
> In gentle inactivity the day.

How many are so far from working with their hands, that they can scarce set a foot to the ground! How many, even young, healthy men, are too lazy either to walk or ride! They must loll in their carriages day by day; and these can scarce be made easy enough! And must not the minor Gentry have their coaches too? Yea, if they only ride on the outside. See here the grand cause (together with intemperance) of our innumerable nervous complaints! For how imperfectly do either medicines or the cold bath supply the place of exercise! without which the human body can no more continue in health than without sleep or food.

We allow likewise the abundant increase of luxury, both

in meat, drink, dress, and furniture. What an amazing profusion of food do we see, not only at a Nobleman's table, but at an ordinary city entertainment; suppose of the Shoemakers' or Tailors' Company! What variety of wines, instead of the good, home-brewed ale, used by our forefathers! What luxury of apparel, changing like the moon, in the city and country, as well as at Court! What superfluity of expensive furniture glitters in all our great men's houses! And luxury naturally increases sloth, unfitting us for exercise either of body or mind. Sloth, on the other hand, by destroying the appetite, leads to still further luxury. And how many does a regular kind of luxury betray at last into gluttony and drunkenness; yea, and lewdness too of every kind; which indeed is hardly separable from them!

An Estimate of the Manners of the Present Times, 1782.

UNGODLINESS THE REAL EVIL

But, allowing all these things, still this is not a true estimate of the present manners of the English nation.

What is the present characteristic of the English nation?

It is ungodliness. This is at present the characteristic of the English nation. Ungodliness is our universal, our constant, our peculiar character.

I do not mean a Deism; the not assenting to revealed religion. No; a Deist is a respectable character compared to an ungodly man. But by ungodliness I mean; First, a total ignorance of God, Secondly, a total contempt of Him.

And, First, a total ignorance of God is almost universal among us. The exceptions are exceeding few, whether among the learned or unlearned. High and low, cobblers, tinkers, hackney-coachmen, men and maid servants, soldiers, sailors, tradesmen of all ranks, Lawyers, Physicians, Gentlemen, Lords, are as ignorant of the Creator of the world as Mahometans or Pagans. They look up to that 'brave o'erhanged firmament, fretted with golden fires'; they see the moon walking in brightness, the sun on his meridian throne; they look around on the various furniture of the earth, herbs, flowers, trees, in all their beauty; and coolly ascribe all to nature, without having any idea affixed to the word. Should you seriously ask them, What is nature? they know not how to answer. Perhaps they will say, 'Why, it is the course of things, that always was, and always will be'. *Always was!* Then you assert that the present course of things was from eternity. If so, the world is eternal; either then there are two eternals, or there is no God!

So much the good people of England in general know of God their Creator!

An Estimate of the Manners of the Present Times, 1782.

Religious Indifference

Again: A vast majority of the English live in the constant neglect of the worship of God. To form a judgement of this, you may take a specimen in the good city of London. How few of the inhabitants worship God in public, even one day a week? Do not yet fewer of them make a conscience of worshipping God in their families? And perhaps they are a still smaller number that daily worship God in their closets. Such, if we acknowledge the truth, is the general, constant ungodliness of the English nation!

An Estimate of the Manners of the Present Times, 1782.

On Sunday Observance

We cannot allow a baker to remain in our society if he sells bread on the Lord's Day. But if he only bakes pies, as they call it, we do not exclude him: although we are convinced that to abstain even from this is the more excellent way.

I am, dear Tommy,
            Your affectionate friend and brother.
                    Letter to Thomas Carlill, May 6, 1785.

. . . To judge whether any action be lawful on the Sabbath or no, we are to consider whether it advances the end for which that was ordained. Now, the end for which the Sabbath was ordained is the attainment of holiness. Whatever therefore tends to advance this end is lawful on this day: whatever does not tend to advance this end is not lawful on this day.

Two things we may infer hence: (1) That works of mercy are lawful on this day; for they directly tend to advance this end, to make us holy as God is holy. (2) That works of necessity are lawful on this day; of which there are two sorts: first, works which we ought to do but cannot do on another day; secondly, works that or works the neglect of which would obstruct this end, for whatever can't be omitted without hindering it do indirectly tend to advance it. One of these, to those who can't perform the offices of religion so well without it, is giving themselves some diversion from it. But of this we may observe that, it being therefore allowed because it tends to advance the end of the day, it is allowable so far and no farther as it does tend to it, to our advance in holiness. It is not enough to say this or that diversion does not obstruct this end; for what does so is allowable on no day: but unless it promotes this particular end, it is not allowable on this day. . . .

Letter to Mrs. Pendarves, April 14, 1731, who had written to Wesley asking him whether she should attend Sunday concerts.

Drink and Poverty: Diverting Corn to Evil Use

But why is food so dear? To come to particulars: Why does bread-corn bear so high a price? To set aside partial causes (which indeed, all put together, are little more than the fly upon the chariot-wheel), the grand cause is, because such immense quantities of corn are continually consumed by distilling. Indeed, an eminent distiller near London, hearing this, warmly replied, 'Nay, my partner and I generally distil but a thousand quarters a week'. Perhaps so. And suppose five-and-twenty distillers, in and near the town, consume each only the same quantity: Here are five-and-twenty thousand quarters a week, that is, above twelve hundred and fifty thousand a year, consumed in and about London! Add the distillers throughout England, and have we not reason to believe, that (not a thirtieth or a twentieth part only, but) little less than half the wheat produced in the kingdom is every year consumed, not by so harmless a way as throwing it into the sea, but by converting it into deadly poison; poison that naturally destroys not only the strength and life, but also the morals, of our countrymen?

Thoughts on the Present Scarcity of Provisions, 1773.

A Legislative Remedy

But how can the price of wheat and barley be reduced? By prohibiting for ever, by making a full end of that bane of health, that destroyer of strength, of life, and of virtue —distilling. Perhaps this alone might go a great way toward answering the whole design. It is not improbable, it would speedily sink the price of corn, at least one part in three. If anything more were required, might not all starch be made of rice, and the importation of this, as well as of corn be encouraged?

Thoughts on the Present Scarcity of Provisions, 1773.

On Banishing Distilled Liquors

Dear Tommy,

Distilled liquors have their use, but are infinitely over-balanced by the abuse of them; therefore, were it in my power, I would banish them out of the world. . . .

I am, dear Tommy,

Your affectionate brother.
Letter to Thomas Wride, December 11, 1787.

Wrestling for the Drunkard's Soul

Are you a man? God made you a man; but you make yourself a beast. Wherein does a man differ from a beast? Is it not chiefly in reason and understanding? But you throw away what reason you have. You strip yourself of your understanding. . . . But that is not all. You make yourself a devil. You stir up all the devilish tempers that are in you, and gain others, which perhaps were not in you; at least you heighten and increase them. You cause the fire of anger, or malice, or lust, to burn seven times hotter than before. At the same time you grieve the Spirit of God, till you drive him quite away from you; and whatever spark of good remained in your soul you drown and quench at once. . . .

I have heard a story of a poor wild Indian, far wiser than either him or you. The English gave him a cask of strong liquor. The next morning he called his friends together, and, setting it in the midst of them, said: 'These white men have given us poison. This man' (calling him by his name) 'was a wise man, and would hurt none but his enemies; but as soon as he had a drink of this, he was mad, and would have killed his own brother. We will not be poisoned.' He then broke the cask, and poured the liquor on the sand.

On what motive do you thus poison yourself? Only for the pleasure of doing it? What, will you make yourself a beast, or rather a devil? . . . Do you not do it for the sake of company? Do you not do it to oblige your friends? For company, do you say? How is this? Will you take a dose of ratsbane for company? But, to oblige your friends? What manner of friends are they who would be obliged by your destroying yourself? Who would suffer, nay entice you so to do? They are villains. They are your worst enemies. They are just such friends, as a man that would smile in your face, and stab you to the heart.

O do not aim at any excuse! Say not, as many do: I am no one's enemy but my own. It is not so. You are an enemy to your King, whom you rob hereby of an useful subject. You are an enemy to your country, which you defraud of the service you might do, either as a man or as a Christian. You are an enemy to every man that sees you in your sin; for your example may move him to do the same. A drunkard is a public enemy. Above all, you are an enemy to God, the great God of heaven and earth. . . . You are setting Him at open defiance. You are an enemy to Christ, to the Lord that bought you. You fly in the face of His authority. You set at nought both His sovereign power and tender love. You crucify Him afresh; and when you call Him your Saviour, what is it less than 'to betray Him with a kiss'.

WESLEY: *A Word to a Drunkard* (*much abridged*).

ON THE USE OF LOTS

I give the same answer to your assertion that we are not ordered in Scripture to decide any points in question by lots. You allow, indeed, there are instances of this in Scripture; but affirm, 'These were miraculous; nor can we without presumption' (a species of enthusiasm) 'apply this method'. I want proof of this: bring one plain text of Scripture, and I am satisfied. 'This I apprehend, you learned from the Moravians!' I did; though, it is true, Mr. Whitefield thought I went too far therein. 'Instances of the same occur in your Journals. I will mention only one. It being debated when you should go to Bristol, you say, "We at length all agreed to decide it by lot. And by this it was determined I should go". Is this your way of carefully considering every step you take? Can there be greater rashness and extravagance? Reason is thus in a manner rendered useless, prudence is set aside, and affairs of moment left to be determined by chance!'

So this you give as a genuine instance of my proceedings; and I suppose, of your own fairness and candour! 'We agreed at length to decide it by lot.' True, at length: after a debate of some hours; after carefully hearing and weighing coolly all the reasons which could be alleged on either side; our brethren still continuing the dispute, without any probability of their coming to one conclusion. 'Can there be greater rashness and extravagance?' I cannot but think there can. 'Reason is thus in a manner rendered useless.' No, we had used it as far as it could go, from Saturday, March 17 (when I received the first letter), to Wednesday, 28, when the case was laid before the Society. 'Prudence is set aside.' Not so, but the arguments here were so equal that she saw not how to determine. 'And affairs of moment left to be determined by chance!' 'By chance!' What a blunder, then, is that, 'The lot is cast into the lap: but the whole disposal thereof is of the Lord'!

This I firmly believe is truth and reason, and will be to the end of the world. And I therefore still subscribe to that declaration of the Moravian Church, laid before the whole body of Divines in the University of Wirtemberg, and not by them accounted enthusiasm: We have a peculiar esteem for lots, and accordingly use them both in public and private to decide points of importance when the reasons brought on each side appear to be of equal weight. And we believe this to be then the only way of wholly setting aside our own will, of acquitting ourselves of all blame, and clearly knowing what is the will of God.

From 'The Principles of a Methodist Farther Explained'. A letter to Thomas Church, 1746.

From a Letter to David Gordon in 1787

I never myself bought a lottery ticket; but I blame not those that do. . . .

The Gaming Churchman

Friend, think a little. What kind of a Churchman is he? A gaming Churchman, a drunken Churchman, a lying Churchman, a cursing and swearing Churchman? . . . For shame! For shame! Do you call a man a Churchman who knows no more of God than a Turk?

A Word to a Freeholder.

The Methodist Standard

My Dear Brother,

I think you misunderstood what a Papist at Lisbon asked a Protestant, 'Do you say I can't be saved in my religion?' He replied, 'I say, Possibly you may be saved in that religion. But I could not'. So I say in the present case to one that asks, 'Can't I be saved if I dance or play at cards?' I answer, 'Possibly you may be saved though you dance and play at cards. But I could not'. So far you may safely speak; but no further. So much and no more I advise our preachers to speak. But I cannot advise them to speak this to unawakened people. It will only anger, not convince them. It is beginning at the wrong end. A plain preacher in London used to say, If you take away his rattles from the child, he will be angry; nay, if he can, he will scratch or bite you. But give him something better first, and he will throw away the rattles of himself. Yet I do not remember that I call these things 'innocent amusements'. And you know we do not suffer any that use them to continue in our Society. Yet I make allowance for *those that are without.* Else I might send my own father and mother to hell, though they not only lived many years, but died in the full assurance of faith.

You do not seem to observe that it has pleased God to give such a measure of light to the Methodists as He has hardly given to any other body of men in the world. And He expects *us* to use all the light we have received, and to deal very tenderly with those who have not received it.

Letter to James Barry, September 26, 1787.

CHAPTER VI

WESLEY, THE EIGHTEENTH-CENTURY CITIZEN

Wesley's religion not only inspired a disciplined use of money
and unceasing private philanthropies, but it also affected his
judgements and activities in regard to public affairs. In this
section we pass from Wesley, the preacher aflame with the love
of God and man, and the organizer of religious societies with
their wide-flung ministries of succour to human need, to Wesley,
the eighteenth-century citizen. Many threads of circumstance
in the condition of the times have to be borne in mind if a fair
and dispassionate judgement is to be passed on Wesley's activity
and influence in this sphere. How did he acquit himself in the
tangle of eighteenth-century affairs, and what was the bearing
of his religious convictions on the judgements he formed and
the attitudes he took?

Labouring under Suspicion

About seven years since, we began preaching inward,
present salvation, as attainable by faith alone.

For preaching this doctrine we were forbidden to preach
in the churches.

We then preached in private houses as occasion offered;
and, when the houses could not contain the people, in the
open air.

For this, many of the Clergy preached or printed against
us, as both heretics and schismatics.

For this, we were represented, both from the pulpit and
the press (we have heard it with our ears, and seen it with
our eyes) as introducing Popery, raising sedition, practising
both against Church and State; and all manner of evil was
publicly said, both of us and those who were accustomed to
meet with us.

*Letter to a Friend, written from Newcastle : Journal, Monday,
    March 11, 1745.*

A Profession of Loyalty

We cannot, indeed, say or do either more or less than we
apprehend consistent with the written Word of God; but

we are ready to obey your Majesty to the uttermost in all things which we conceive to be agreeable thereto. And we earnestly exhort all with whom we converse, as they fear God, to honour the King. We of the clergy in particular put all men in mind to revere the higher powers as of God; and continually declare, 'Ye must needs be subject, not only for wrath, but also for conscience' sake'.

Silver and gold (most of us must own) we have none; but such as we have we humbly beg your Majesty to accept together with our hearts and prayers. May He who hath bought us with His blood, the Prince of all the kings of the earth, fight against all the enemies of your Majesty with the two-edged sword that cometh out of His mouth! And when He calleth your Majesty from his throne, full of years and victories, may it be with that voice, 'Come, receive the kingdom prepared for thee from the beginning of the world!'

These are the continual prayers of your Majesty's dutiful and loyal subjects.

Letter to George II, March 5, 1744.

At Newcastle, when Rebellion Threatened

About five we came to Newcastle, in an acceptable time. We found the generality of the inhabitants in the utmost consternation, news being just arrived that, the morning before, at two o'clock, the Pretender had entered Edinburgh. A great concourse of people were with us in the evening, to whom I expounded the third Chapter of Jonah; insisting particularly on that verse, 'Who can tell, if God will return, and repent, and turn away from his fierce anger, that we perish not?'

The Mayor (Mr. Ridley) summoned all the householders of the town to meet him at the Town Hall; and desired as many of them as were willing to set their hands to a paper, importing that they would, at the hazard of their goods and lives, defend the town against the common enemy. Fear and darkness were now on every side; but not on those who had seen the light of God's countenance. We rejoiced together in the evening with solemn joy, while God applied those words to many hearts: 'Fear not, ye; for I know that ye seek Jesus, which was crucified.'

The Mayor ordered the townsmen to be under arms, and to mount guard in their turns, over and above the guard of soldiers; a few companies of whom had been drawn into the town on the first alarm. Now, also, Pilgrim-street Gate was ordered to be walled up. Many began to be much concerned for *us*, because our house stood without walls. Nay, but the Lord is a wall of fire unto all that trust in Him.

I had desired all our brethren to join with us this day in seeking God by fasting and prayer. About one we met, and poured out our souls before Him; and we believed He would send an answer of peace.

Journal, Wednesday, September 18—*Friday, September* 20, 1745.

LETTER TO THE MAYOR OF NEWCASTLE

The same day the action was, came the news of General Cope's defeat. Orders were now given for the doubling of the guard, and for walling up Pandon and Sally-Port Gates. In the afternoon I wrote the following letter:—

To the Worshipful the Mayor of Newcastle.

SIR,

My not waiting upon you at the Town Hall was not owing to any want of respect. I reverence you for your office sake, and much more for your zeal in the execution of it. I would to God every magistrate in the land would copy after such an example! Much less was it owing to any disaffection to His Majesty King George: but I knew not how far it might be either necessary or proper for me to appear on such an occasion. I have no fortune at Newcastle: I have only the bread I eat, and the use of a little room for a few weeks in the year.

All I can do for His Majesty, whom I honour and love, I think, not less than I did my own father, is this: I cry unto God day by day, in public and in private, to put all his enemies to confusion; and I exhort all that hear me to do the same, and, in their several stations, to exert themselves as loyal subjects, who, so long as they fear God, cannot but honour the King.

Permit me, Sir, to add a few words more, out of the

fulness of my heart. I am persuaded that you fear God, and
have a deep sense that his kingdom ruleth over all. Unto
whom, then (I may ask you) should we flee for succour,
but unto Him whom, by our sins, we have justly displeased?
O, Sir, is it not possible to give any check to these over-
flowings of ungodliness?—to the open, flagrant wickedness,
the drunkenness and profaneness, which so abound, even
in our streets? I just take leave to suggest this. May the
God whom you serve direct you in this and all things!
This is the daily prayer of,

Sir,

Your obedient Servant, for Christ's sake.

J.W.

Midst War's Alarms

Advice came that they (the young Pretender's forces)
were in full march southward, so that it was supposed they
would reach Newcastle by Monday evening. At eight I
called on a multitude of sinners in Gateshead, to seek the
Lord while he might be found. Mr. Ellison preached
another earnest sermon, and all the people seemed to bend
before the Lord. In the afternoon I expounded part of the
lesson for the day, Jacob wrestling with the Angel. The
congregation was so moved, that I began again and again,
and knew not how to conclude; and we cried mightily to
God to send His Majesty King George help from his holy
place, and to spare a sinful land yet a little longer, if haply
they might know the day of their visitation.

Journal, Sunday, September 29, 1745.

Concerning the Pretender

Do you ever think? Do you ever consider? If not, it is
high time you should. Think a little, before it is too late.
Consider what a state you are in; and not you alone, but
our whole nation. We would have war; and we have had
it. And what is the fruit? Our armies broken in pieces;
and thousands of our men either killed on the spot, or
made prisoners in one day. Nor is this all. We have now
war at our own doors; our own countrymen turning their
swords against their brethren. And have any hitherto
been able to stand before them? Have they not already

seized upon one whole kingdom? Friend, either think now, or sleep on and take your rest, till you drop into the pit where you will sleep more.

Think what is likely to follow, if an army of French also should blow the trumpet in our land! What desolation may we not then expect? what a wide-spread field of blood? And what can the end of these things be? If they prevail, what but Popery and slavery? Do you know what the spirit of Popery is? Did you never hear of that in Queen Mary's reign; and of the holy men who were then burned alive by the Papists, because they did not dare to do as they did; to worship angels and saints, to pray to the Virgin Mary, to bow down to images, and the like? If we had a King of this spirit, whose life would be safe? at least, what honest man's? A knave indeed might turn with the times. But what a dreadful thing would this be to a man of conscience. 'Either turn or burn: Either go into that fire, or into "the fire that never shall be quenched"!'

A Word in Season; or Advice to an Englishman, 1744–5.

A Call to Repentance

Brethren, countrymen, Englishmen, what shall we do; to-day, while it is called to-day, before the season of mercy is quite expired, and our 'destruction cometh as a whirlwind'? Which way can we remove the evils we feel? which way prevent those we fear? Is there any better way than the making God our friend? the securing his help against our enemies? Other helps are little worth. We see armies may be destroyed, or even flee away from old men and children. Fleets may be dashed to pieces in an hour, and sunk in the depths of the sea. Allies may be treacherous, or slow, or foolish, or weak, or cowardly; but God is a friend who cannot betray, and whom none can either bribe or terrify. And who is wise, or swift, or strong like him? Therefore, whatever we do, let us make God our friend; let us with all speed remove the cause of his anger; let us cast away our sins. Then shall his love have free course, and he will send us help, sufficient help, against all our enemies.

A Word in Season; or Advice to an Englishman 1744-5.

A Voter's Duty

What are you going to do? to vote for a Parliament man? I hope then you have taken no money. For doubtless you know the strictness of the oath—that you have received no 'gift or reward, directly or indirectly, nor any promise of any, on account of your vote' in the ensuing election. Surely you start at perjury! at calm, fore-thought, deliberate, wilful perjury! If you are guilty already, stop; go no farther. It is at the peril of your soul. Will you sell your God, your Saviour? Nay, God forbid! Rather cast down just now the thirty pieces of silver or gold, and say, 'Sir, I will not sell heaven. Neither you nor all the world is able to pay the purchase'.

I hope you have received nothing else, neither will receive; no entertainment, no meat or drink. If this is given you on account of your vote, you are perjured still. How can you make oath, you have received no gift? This was a gift, if you did not buy it. What! will you sell your soul to the devil for a draught of drink, or for a morsel of bread? O consider what you do! Act as if the whole election depended on your single vote, and as if the whole Parliament depended (and therein the whole nation) on that single person whom you now choose to be a member of it.

But if you take nothing of any, for whom shall you vote? For the man that loves God. He must love his country, and that from a steady, invariable principle. And by his fruits you shall know him. He is careful to abstain from all appearance of evil. He is zealous of good works, as he has opportunity, doing good to all men. He uses all the ordinances of God, and that both constantly and carefully. And he does this, not barely as something he must do, or what he would willingly be excused from; no, he rejoices in this his reasonable service, as a blessed privilege of the children of God.

But what, if none of the candidates have these fruits? Then vote for him that loves the King, King George, whom the wise providence of God has appointed to reign over us. He ought to be highly esteemed in love, even for his office sake. A King is a lovely, sacred name. He is a minister of God unto thee for good. How much more such a King, as has been, in many respects, a blessing to his subjects! You may easily know those who love him not; for they generally glory in their shame. They 'are not afraid to speak evil of dignities'; no, not even of the 'ruler of their people'.

Perhaps you will say, 'But I love my country; therefore I am for the country interest'. I fear you know not what you say. Are you against your King because you love your country? Who taught you to separate your King from your country? to set one against the other? Be assured, none that loves either. True lovers of their country do not talk in this senseless manner.

Is not the interest of the King of England, and of the country of England, one and the same? If the King is destroyed, doth it profit the country? If the country, does it profit the King? Their interest cannot be divided. The welfare of one is the welfare of both.

Have you any objection of a different kind? Do you say, 'I am for the Church? The Church of England for ever! Therefore I vote for . . .; he is a true Churchman, a lover of the Church'. Are you sure of that? Friend, think a little. What kind of a Churchman is he? a whoring Churchman, a gaming Churchman, a drunken Churchman, a lying Churchman, a cursing and swearing Churchman? or a red-hot persecuting Churchman, that would send all Dissenters to the devil at a clap? For shame! for shame! Do you call a man a Churchman, who knows no more of God than a Turk? call a man a Churchman, that does not even pretend to so much religion as would serve an honest Heathen? He is a lover of the Church who is a lover of God, and consequently of all mankind. Whoever else talks of loving the Church, is a cheat. Set a mark upon that man.

Above all, mark that man who talks of loving the Church, and does not love the King. If he does not love the King, he cannot love God. And if he does not love God, he cannot love the Church. He loves the Church and the King just alike. For indeed he loves neither one nor the other.

O beware, you who truly love the Church, and therefore cannot but love the King; beware of dividing the King and the Church, any more than the King and country. Let others do as they will, what is that to you? Act you as an honest man, a loyal subject, a true Englishman, a lover of

the country, a lover of the Church; in one word, a Christian!
one that fears nothing but sin, that seeks nothing but
heaven, and that desires nothing but God; nothing but
glory to God in the highest, and on earth peace, good-will
towards men!   *A Word to a Freeholder.*

(Many thousands of this pamphlet were printed and
distributed in Wesley's lifetime.)

At a Cornish Election: St. Ives, 1747

Tuesday 30. We came to St. Ives before morning prayers,
and walked to church without so much as one huzza. How
strangely has one year changed the scene in Cornwall.

Wednesday, July 1. I spoke severally to all those who had
votes in the ensuing election. I found them such as I
desired; not one would even eat or drink at the expense
of him for whom he voted. Five guineas had been given to
W.C., but he returned them immediately; T.M. positively
refused to accept any thing; and when he heard that his
mother had received money privately, he could not rest
till she gave him the three guineas, which he instantly sent
back.

Thursday the 2nd was the day of election for Parliament-
men. It was begun and ended without any hurry at all. I
had a large congregation in the evening, among whom
two or three roared for the disquietness of their heart; as did
many at the meeting which followed, particularly those who
had lost their first love.

Journal, Tuesday, June 30, to Thursday, July 2, 1747.

Concerning another Election

Dear Sir,

If the election of Mr. Spencer be a thing of any consequence, then it was extremely ill-judged to prevent his
coming down. He ought to have been here at all hazards,
if he was not very dangerously ill. His absence will probably
turn the scale; and if the Jacobites gain one member now,
they will have two the next time. Whereas there is reason
to believe had Mr. Spencer appeared, there would have
been no opposition.

E

Last night I desired all the freemen of our Society to meet me after preaching, and enlarged a little upon His Majesty's character and the reasons we had to spare no pains in his service. I believe all who had been wavering were fully convinced. But some had absolutely promised to vote for Mr. Smith, it having been confidently reported that both the candidates were equally acceptable to His Majesty.

The whole city is in confusion. Oh what pity there could not be some way of managing elections of every sort without this embittering Englishmen against Englishmen and kindling fires which cannot be quenched in many years!

Letter to Ebenezer Blackwell, March 4, 1756.

ADVICE TO ELECTORS

MY DEAR BROTHER,

If, as I am informed, Mr. Gregor is a lover of King George and the present Administration, I wish you would advise all our brethren that have votes to assist him in the ensuing election.

I am,

Your affectionate friend and brother.

Letter to John Mason, 1789.

THE MIND OF THE METHODIST CONFERENCE

Extirpate bribery, receiving anything directly or indirectly, for voting in any election.

Conference : 1763.

Q.31: How may bribery be prevented at the ensuing elections?

Answer: (1) Show the wickedness of selling our country, in every Society.

(2) Do the same in private conversation.

(3) Read *Word to a Freeholder* and disperse it with both hands. But a voter may suffer his expenses to be borne and bear no blame.

Conference, 1767.

Concern for Purity in Public Life

*To all who have had East India stock lately transferred to them,
in order to qualify them for voting at the election for directors on
Wednesday next.*

GENTLEMEN AND LADIES,

Do you know what the oath is which you are to take before
you will be admitted to vote? It is as follows: 'I, A.B., do
swear that the sum of five hundred pounds, or more, of the
capital stock of the United Company of Merchants of
England trading to the East Indies doth at this time belong
to me in my own right, and not in trust for any other person
or persons whatsoever. So help me God.'

Do not you hereby call upon God either to help you or
to send down His curse upon you as your oath is true or
false?

If you consider this, can you take a false oath? can you
call God to witness to a lie?

Are you not doing this if the stock standing in your name
is not your real and true property?

Have you not given a note of your hand for it, which is
to be returned upon your retransferring the stock?

Are you either benefited or hurt by the rise or fall of the
stock? If not, can you say you are proprietor at all?

Does it alter the case, though a third person lend you the
money to pay for that stock which you are so to retransfer?
Still you neither gain nor lose by the rise or fall of the stock:
a plain proof that you have no property therein.

Weigh this in time; and do not, to oblige a friend, bring
the guilt of perjury on your own soul.

Letter to certain Proprietors of East India Stock, September, 1773.
(This letter is explained by the fraudulent transfer of stock
temporarily or in trust to enable certain persons to qualify
as voters.)

BRISTOL 1774

Thursday 6. I met those of our Society who had votes
in the ensuing election, and advised them (1) to vote,
without fee or reward, for the person they judged most

worthy; (2) to speak no evil of the person they voted against; and (3) to take care their spirits were not sharpened against those that voted on the other side.

Journal ; Thursday, October 6, 1774.

(The occasion of Edmund Burke's first candidature and election as member for Bristol.)

Wesley and the Wreckers of Cornwall

I was afterwards inquiring, if that scandal of Cornwall, the plundering of wrecked vessels, still subsisted? He said, 'As much as ever; only the Methodists will have nothing to do with it. But three months since, a vessel was wrecked on the south coast, and the tinners presently seized on all the goods; and even broke in pieces a new coach which was on board, and carried every scrap of it away'. But is there no way to prevent this shameful breach of all the laws, both of religion and humanity? Indeed there is. The gentry of Cornwall may totally prevent it whenever they please. Let them only see that the laws be strictly executed upon the next plunderers; and after an example is made of ten of these, the next wreck will be unmolested. Nay, there is a milder way. Let them only agree together, to discharge any tinner or labourer that is concerned in the plundering of a wreck, and advertise his name, that no Cornish gentleman may employ him any more; and neither tinner nor labourer will any more be concerned in that bad work.   *Journal, Port Isaac, Saturday, August* 17, 1776.

Smuggling, Unpatriotic and Unchristian

'What is smuggling?' It is the importing, selling, or buying of run goods; that is, those which have not paid the duty appointed by law to be paid to the King.

What harm is there in it?

I answer, open smuggling (such as was common a few years ago, on the southern coasts especially) is robbing on the highway; and as much harm as there is in this, just so much there is in smuggling. A smuggler of this kind is no honester than an highwayman. They may shake hands together.

Private smuggling is just the same with picking pockets. There is fully as much harm in this as in that. A smuggler of this kind is no honester than a pickpocket. These may shake hands together.

But open smugglers are worse than common pickpockets. For it is undoubtedly worse to rob our father than one we have no obligation to. And it is worse still, far worse, to rob a good father, one who sincerely loves us, and is at that very time doing all he can to provide for us and to make us happy. Now this is exactly the present case. King George is the father of all his subjects; and not only so, but he is a good father. He shows his love to them on all occasions; and is continually doing all that is in his power to make his subjects happy.

If you believe the Bible, I say to you, as our Saviour said to them of old time, 'Render unto Cæsar the things that are Cæsar's and unto God the things that are God's'. If then you mind our Saviour's words, be as careful to honour the King as to fear God. Be as exact in giving the King what is due to the King, as in giving God what is due to God. Upon no account whatever rob or defraud him of the least thing which is his lawful property.

If you believe the Bible, I say to you, as St. Paul said to the ancient Christians, 'Render unto all their dues; in particular, custom to whom custom is due, tribute to whom tribute'. Now, custom is by the laws of England due to the King; therefore every one in England is bound to pay it him. So that robbing the King herein is abundantly worse than common stealing, or common robbing on the highway.

And so it is on another account also: for it is a general robbery: It is, in effect, not only robbing the King, but robbing every honest man in the nation. For the more the King's duties are diminished, the more the taxes must be increased. And these lie upon us all; they are the burden, not of some, but of all the people of England. Therefore every smuggler is a thief-general, who picks the pockets both of the King and all his fellow-subjects. He wrongs them all; and, above all, the honest traders; many of whom he deprives of their maintenance; constraining them either not to sell their goods at all, or to sell them to no profit. Some of them are tempted hereby, finding they cannot get bread for their families, to turn thieves too. And then you are accountable for their sin as well as your own; you bring their blood upon your own head. Calmly consider this, and you will never more ask what harm there is in smuggling.

A Word to a Smuggler, 1767.

Conference Discusses It

Q. How may smuggling be abolished?

Answer: Speak tenderly and frequently of it in every Society near the coast.

Carefully disperse the *Word to a Smuggler*.

Expel all who will not leave it off.

Silence every local preacher that defends it.

Smugglers at Sunderland

Saturday 23. I spoke to each of the Society in Sunderland. Most of the robbers, commonly called Smugglers, have left us; but more than twice the number of honest people are already come in their place: and if none had come, yet should I not dare to keep those who steal either from the King or subject.

Journal, Sunderland, June 23, 1759.

Robbing the King at Dover

Tuesday 3. I rode to Dover, and found a little company more united together than they have been for many years. Whilst several of them continued to rob the King, we seemed to be ploughing the sand. But since they have cut off the right hand, the word of God sinks deep into their hearts.

Journal, Dover, Tuesday, December 3, 1765.

Chapter VII

WESLEY'S POLITICAL PRINCIPLES

WESLEY exerted considerable influence in forming and directing public opinion during the eighteenth century. He was a political pamphleteer with whom party politicians had on occasion to reckon. On what principles did he form his judgements on current affairs, how far did he consider it his duty to speak, and what idea of political power and authority did he hold?

Several of his pamphlets supply the answers. One of the shortest and most revealing is one entitled: *How far is it the Duty of a Christian Minister to Preach Politics?* We learn from it how deep-rooted was Wesley's loyalty to King and Government. Other important pamphlets were evoked by the famous case of John Wilkes, which kept political England in a ferment for at least a decade: 1763–1774. Wilkes' arrest under a general warrant for attacking the government, and later Parliament's refusal to admit him after election as member for Middlesex, aroused fierce political passions. The Letters of Junius stirred the public mind. 'Wilkes and Liberty' was the cry, and crowds broke into riotous behaviour. Wilkes was a worthless character, but his case served, as sometimes happens, for political advance. The usurpation of illegal powers by the Commons was frustrated and a blow was struck for Parliamentary reform, while a great judge declared general warrants illegal. Wesley's contributions to the debate were two: *Free Thoughts on Public Affairs*, 1768, and *Thoughts on Liberty*, 1772. As the extracts indicate, he showed himself suspicious of political agitation, sensitive to the perils of mob-law, keen about religious and civil liberty, but not sensible of any need of greater political liberty. An extension even of the very limited franchise of that day would probably have seemed to him not only unnecessary, but undesirable. A final extract from *Thoughts concerning the Origin of Power* shows his attitude to the political doctrine which John Locke had made so popular, viz: that all political authority is derived from the people. This Wesley strenuously denied. Power, he declared, comes from God.

RELIGION AND POLITICS: LOYALTY TO THE KING

It is impossible to answer this question before it is understood. We must, First, therefore endeavour to understand it; and then it will be easy to answer.

There is a plain command in the Bible, 'Thou shalt not speak evil of the ruler of the people'. But notwithstanding this, many that are called religious people speak evil of him continually. And they speak many things that are palpably false; particularly when they affirm him to be a weak man; whereas a Nobleman, who is not at all prejudiced in his favour, when he was pressed to speak, made this honest declaration: 'Sir, I know him well; and I judge the King to be one of the most sensible men in Europe. His Ministers are no fools; but His Majesty is able to wind them all round his finger.'

Now, when a Clergyman comes into a place where this and many more stories, equally false, have been diligently propagated against the King, and are generally believed, if he guards the people against this evil-speaking, by refuting those slanders, many cry out, 'O, he is preaching politics!'

If you mean this by the term, it is the bounden duty of every Christian Minister to preach politics. It is our bounden duty to refute these vile aspersions, in public as well as in private. But this can be done only now and then, when it comes naturally in our way. For it is our main and constant business to 'preach Jesus Christ, and him crucified'.

Again: Many who do not so freely censure the King, speak all manner of evil of his Ministers. If any misfortune befalls us at home or abroad, by sea or land, it is 'all their fault'. If one commander in America is surprised with all his forces when he is dead drunk, 'Lord North deserves to be hanged'. If General Burgoyne or Lord Cornwallis is betrayed into their enemy's hand, all the blame is laid on our Ministers at home. But still the King is wounded through their sides; the blame glances from them to him. Yet if we say a word in defence of them (which is in effect defending him), this also is preaching politics.

It is always difficult and frequently impossible for private men to judge of the measures taken by men in public offices. We do not see many of the grounds which determine them to act in this or the contrary manner. Generally, therefore, it behoves us to be silent, as we may suppose they know their own business best; but when they are censured without any colour of reason, and when an odium is cast on the King by that means, we ought to preach politics in this sense also; we ought publicly to confute those unjust censures: Only remembering still, that this is rarely to be done, and only when fit occasion offers; it being our main business to preach 'repentance towards God, and faith in our Lord Jesus Christ'.

LEWISHAM, January 9, 1782.

How far is it the Duty of a Christian Minister to Preach Politics? 1782.

ON FORMING POLITICAL JUDGEMENTS

You desire me to give you my thoughts freely on the present state of public affairs. But do you consider? I am no politician; politics lie quite out of my province. Neither have I any acquaintance, at least no intimacy, with any that bear that character. And it is no easy matter to form any judgement concerning things of so complicated a nature. It is the more difficult, because, in order to form our judgement, such a multitude of facts should be known, few of which can be known with tolerable exactness by any but those who are eye-witnesses of them. And how few of these will relate what they have seen precisely as it was, without adding, omitting, or altering any circumstance, either with or without design! And may not a slight addition or alteration give a quite different colour to the whole?

And as we cannot easily know, with any accuracy, the facts on which we are chiefly to form our judgement; so, much less can we expect to know the various springs of action which gave rise to those facts, and on which, more than on the bare actions themselves, the characters of the actors depend. It is on this account that an old writer advises us to judge nothing before the time; to abstain, as far as possible, from judging peremptorily, either of things or persons, till the time comes, when 'the hidden things of darkness', the facts now concealed, 'will be brought to light', and the hidden springs of action will be discovered—'the thoughts and intents of every human heart'.

Perhaps you will say, 'Nay, every Englishman is a politician; we suck in politics with our mother's milk. It is as natural for us to talk politics as to breathe; we can instruct both the King and his Council. We can in a trice reform the State, point out every blunder of this or that Minister, and tell every step they ought to take to be arbiters of all Europe'.

I grant, every cobbler, tinker, porter, and hackney-coachman can do this; but I am not so deep learned. While they are sure of everything, I am in a manner sure of nothing; except of that very little which I see with my own eyes, or hear with my own ears. However, since you desire me to tell you what I think, I will do it with all openness. Only please to remember, I do not take upon me to dictate either to you or to any one. I only use the privilege of an Englishman, to speak my naked thoughts; setting down just what appears to me to be the truth, till I have better information. At present, indeed, I have not much information, having read little upon this head but the public papers; and you know these are mostly on one side; in them little is to be seen on the other side; and that little is seldom wrote by masterly writers. How few of them have such a pen as Junius!

But supposing we have ever so much information, how little can one rely on it! on the information given by either party! For is not one as warm as the other? And who does not know how impossible it is for a man to see things right when he is angry? Does not passion blind the eyes of the understanding, as smoke does the bodily eyes? And how little of the truth can we learn from those who see nothing but through a cloud?

This advantage then I have over both parties—the being angry at neither. So that if I have a little understanding from nature or experience, it is (in this instance at least) unclouded by passion. I wish the same happiness which I wish to myself, to those on one side and on the other. I would not hurt either in the least degree; I would not willingly give them any pain.

I have likewise another advantage, that of having no bias one way or the other. I have no interest depending; I want no man's favour, having no hopes, no fears, from any man; and having no particular attachment of any kind to either of the contending parties.

But am I so weak as to imagine, that because I am not angry at them, they will not be angry at me? No; I do not imagine any such thing. Probably both will be angry enough; that is the warm men on both sides, were it only for this—that I am not as warm as themselves. For what is more insufferable to a man in a passion, than to see you keep your temper? And is it not a further provocation, that I do not behave as he does to his opponent; that I call him no ill names; that I give him no ill words? I expect, therefore, to be abused on all sides; and cannot be disappointed, unless by being treated with common humanity.

Free Thoughts on Public Affairs, 1770.

Under Which King?

'But what do you think the end will be?' It is easy to foresee this. Supposing things to take their natural course, they must go from bad to worse.

> *In stipulam veluti cum flamma furentibus Austris*
> *Incidit, aut rapidus montano flumine torrens*
> *Exiit, oppositasque evicit gurgite moles.*

The people will be inflamed more and more; the torrent will swell higher and higher, till at length it bursts through all opposition, and overflows the land. The consequences of these commotions will be (unless an higher hand interpose) exactly the same as those of the like commotions in the last century. First, the land will become a field of blood; many thousands of poor Englishmen will sheathe their swords in each other's bowels, for the diversion of their good neighbours. Then either a commonwealth will ensue, or else a second Cromwell. One must be; but it cannot be determined which, King W—— or King Mob.

'But that case is not parallel with this.' It is not, in all particulars. In many respects it is widely different. As, First, with regard to the King himself. Few will affirm the character of King Charles, even allowing the account given by Lord Clarendon to be punctually true in every respect, to be as faultless as that of King George. But other passions, as well as love, are blind. So that when these are raised to a proper height, especially when Junius has thrown a little more of his magic dust into the eyes of the people, and convinced them that what are virtues in others, are mere vices in him, the good patriots will see no manner of difference between a King George and King Charles, or even a Nero.

Free Thoughts on Public Affairs, 1770.

ALL MEN DESIRE LIBERTY

All men in the world desire liberty; whoever breathes, breathes after this, and that by a kind of natural instinct antecedent to art or education. Yet at the same time all men of understanding acknowledge it is a rational instinct. For we feel this desire, not in opposition to, but in consequence of, our reason. Therefore it is not found, or in a very low degree, in many species of brutes, which seem, even when they are left to their choice, to prefer servitude before liberty.

The love of liberty is then the glory of rational beings; and it is the glory of Britons in particular. Perhaps it would be difficult to find any nation under heaven, who are more tenacious of it; nay, it may be doubted if any nation ever was; not the Spartans, not the Athenians; no, not the Romans themselves, who have been celebrated for this very thing by the poets and historians of all ages.

Such was the sense of all our ancestors, even from the earliest ages. And is it not also the general sense of the nation at this day? Who can deny that the whole kingdom is panting for liberty? Is not the cry for it gone forth, not only through every part of our vast metropolis—from the west end of the city to the east, from the north to the south, so that instead of no complaining in our streets, there is nothing but complaining—but likewise into every corner of our land, borne by all the four winds of heaven? Liberty! Liberty! sounds through every county, every city, every town, and every hamlet!

Thoughts upon Liberty, 1772.

TRUE LIBERTY! RELIGIOUS AND CIVIL

But to speak seriously. These things being set aside, which the bawling mob dignify by that name; what is that liberty, properly so called, which every wise and good man desires? It is either religious or civil. Religious liberty is a liberty to choose our own religion, to worship God according to our own conscience, according to the best light we have. Every man living, as man, has a right to this, as he is a rational creature. The Creator gave him this right when he endowed him with understanding. And every man must judge for himself, because every man must give an account of himself to God.

Consequently, this is an indefeasible right; it is inseparable from humanity. And God did never give authority to any man, or number of men, to deprive any child of man thereof, under any colour or pretence whatever. What an amazing thing is it, then, that the governing part of almost every nation under heaven should have taken upon them, in all ages, to rob all under their power of this liberty! yea, should take upon them, at this day, so to do! to force rational creatures into their own religion! Would one think it possible that the most sensible men in the world should say to their fellow-creatures, 'Either be of my religion, or I will take away your food, and you and your wife and children shall starve: If that will not convince you, I will fetter your hands and feet, and throw you into a dungeon: And if still you will not see as I see, I will burn you alive'?

It would not be altogether so astonishing if this were the manner of American savages. But what shall we say if numberless instances of it have occurred in the politest nations of Europe? Have no instances of the kind been seen in Britain? Have not England and Scotland seen the horrid fires? Have not the flames burning the flesh of heretics shone in London as well as in Paris and Lisbon? Have we forgot the days of good Queen Mary? No; they will be had in everlasting remembrance. And although burning was out of fashion in Queen Elizabeth's days, yet hanging, even for religion, was not. It is true, her successor did not go quite so far. But did even King James allow liberty of conscience? By no means. During his whole reign, what liberty had the Puritans? What liberty had they in the following reign? If they were not persecuted unto death (although eventually, indeed, many of them were; for they died in their imprisonment); yet were they not continually harassed by prosecution in the Bishops' Courts, or Star-Chamber? by fines upon fines, frequently reducing them to deepest poverty? and by imprisonment for months, yea for years together, till many of them, escaping with the skin of their teeth, left their country and friends, fled to seek their bread in the wilds of America? 'However, we may suppose all this was at an end under the merry Monarch, King Charles the Second.' Was it indeed? Where have they lived who suppose this? To wave a thousand particular instances; what will you say to those two public monuments, the Act of Uniformity, and the Act against Conventicles? In the former it is enacted, to the eternal honour of the King, Lords, and Commons, at that memorable period: 'Every Parson, Vicar, or other Minister whatever, who has any benefice within these realms, shall, before the next twenty-fourth of August, openly and publicly declare his unfeigned assent and consent to all and everything contained in the Book of Common Prayer, or shall, *ipso facto*, be deprived of all his benefices! Likewise, if any Dean, Prebendary, Master, Fellow, Chaplain, or Tutor, of any College, Hall, House of Learning, or Hospital, any public Professor, or any other person in Holy Orders, any Schoolmaster, or Teacher, or Tutor in any private family, do not subscribe hereto, he shall be, *ipso facto*, deprived of his place, and shall be utterly disabled from continuing therein.'

Property for ever! See how well English property was secured in those golden days!

So, by this glorious Act, thousands of men, guilty of no crime, nothing contrary either to justice, mercy, or truth, were stripped of all they had, of their houses, lands, revenues, and driven to seek, where they could, or beg their bread. For what? Because they did not dare to worship God according to other men's consciences! So they and their families were, at one stroke, turned out of house and home, and reduced to little less than beggary, for no other fault, real or pretended, but because they could not assent and consent to that manner of worship which their worthy governors prescribed!

But this was not all. It was further enacted by the same merciful lawgivers: 'If any person act as a Teacher, Tutor, or Schoolmaster, in any private family, before he has subscribed hereto, he shall suffer three months' imprisonment, without bail or mainprize.'

Liberty for ever! Here is security for your person, as well as your property.

By virtue of the Act against Conventicles, if any continued to worship God according to their own conscience, they were first robbed of their substance, and, if they persisted, of their liberty; often of their lives also. For this crime, under this 'our most religious and gracious King' (what were they who publicly told God he was such?), Englishmen were not only spoiled of their goods, but denied even the use of the free air, yea, and the light of the sun, being thrust by hundreds into dark and loathsome prisons!

Thoughts upon Liberty, 1772.

UNDER KING GEORGE: IS LIBERTY DENIED?

But is this the case at present with us? Are we abridged of our religious liberty? His late Majesty was desired, about thirty years ago, to take a step of this kind. But his answer was worthy of a King, yes, the King of a free people: 'I tell you, while I sit on the English throne, no man shall be persecuted for conscience's sake.' And it is certain he made his promise good from the beginning of his reign to the end. But perhaps the case is altered now. Does His present Majesty tread in his steps? He does, he persecutes no man for conscience's sake. If he does, where is the man? I do not ask, Whom has he committed to the flames, or caused to die by the common hangman? or, Whom has he caused to die many deaths, by hunger and thirst, cold and nakedness? but, Whom has he tortured or thrust into a dungeon, yea, or imprisoned at all, or fined, for worshipping God according to his own conscience, in the Presbyterian or any other way? O, compare King Charles, gracious Charles the Second, with King George, and you will know the value of the liberty you enjoy.

In the name of wonder, what religious liberty can you desire, or even conceive, which you have not already? Where is there a nation in Europe, in the habitable world, which enjoys such liberty of conscience as the English? I will be bold to say there is nothing like it in Holland, in Germany (Protestant or Popish), in either the Protestant or Popish cantons of Switzerland; no, nor in any country under the sun. Have we not in England full liberty to choose any religion, yea, or no religion at all? to have no more religion than a Hottentot, shall I say? nay, no more than a bull or a swine? Whoever therefore in England stretches his throat, and bawls for more religious liberty, must be totally void of shame, and can have no excuse but want of understanding.

But is not the ground of this vehement outcry, that we are deprived of our civil liberty? What is civil liberty? A liberty to enjoy our lives and fortunes in our own way; to use our property, whatever is legally our own, according to our own choice. And can you deny, 'that we are robbed of this liberty'? Who are? Certainly I am not. I pray, do not face me down as I am. Do not argue me out of my senses. If the Great Turk, or the King of France, wills that a man should die, with or without cause, die he must. And instances of the kind continually occur; but no such instances occur in England. I am in no more danger of death from King George, than from the Queen of Hungary. And if I study to be quiet and mind my own business, I am in no more danger of losing my liberty than my life. No, nor my property; I mean by any act of the King. If this is in any degree invaded, it is not by the King, or his Parliament, or army, but by the good patriots.

Hark! Is hell or Bedlam broke loose? What roaring is that, loud as the waves of the sea? 'It is the patriot mob.' What do they want with me? Why do they flock about my house? 'Make haste! illuminate your windows in honour of Mr. Wilkes.' I cannot in conscience; I think it is encouraging vice. 'Then they will all be broken.' That is, in plain English, Give them twenty shillings, or they will rob you of five pounds. Here are champions for the laws of the land! for liberty and property! O vile horse-guards!

> That dared, so grim and terrible, to'advance
> Their miscreated fronts athwart the way!

True, they did nothing and said nothing. Yet, in default of the civil powers, who did not concern themselves with the matter, they hindered the mob from finishing their work.

Why, then, these men, instead of anyway abridging it, plainly preserved my liberty and property. And by their benefit, not the care of these to whom it properly belonged, I still enjoy full civil liberty. I am free to live, in every respect, according to my own choice. My life, my person, my property, are safe. I am not murdered, maimed, tortured at any man's pleasure; I am not thrown into prison; I am not manacled; see, I have not one fetter, either on my hands or feet. And are not you as free as I am? Are not you at liberty to enjoy the fruit of your labours? Who hinders you from doing it? Does King George? Does Lord North? Do any of His Majesty's officers or soldiers? No, nor any man living. Perhaps some would hinder you, if you acted contrary to law; but this is not liberty, it is licentiousness. Deny the fact who can, am not I free to use my substance according to my own discretion? And do not you enjoy the self-same freedom? You cannot, you dare not deny it. At this hour I am at full liberty to use my property as I please. And so are you; you do, in fact, use your house, your goods, your land, as is right in your own eyes. Does anyone take them from you? No; nor does anyone restrain you from the full enjoyment of them. What then is the matter? What is it you are making all this pother about? Why are you thus wringing your hands, and screaming, to the terror of your quiet neighbours, 'Destruction! slavery! bondage! Help, countrymen! our liberty is destroyed! We are ruined, chained, fettered, undone!' *Fettered!* How? Where are the fetters, but in your own imagination? There are none, either on your hands or mine; Neither you nor I can show to any man in his senses, that we have one chain upon us, even so big as a knitting-needle.

Thoughts upon Liberty, 1772.

JOHN WILKES AND LIBERTY

Is it not for the sake of this, that the name of our great patriot (perhaps not so admirable in his private character as the man of Ross, or so great a lover of his country as Codrus or old Curtius) is more celebrated than that of any private man has been in England for these thousand years; that his very picture is so joyfully received in every part of England and Ireland; that we stamp his (I had almost said, adored) name on our handkerchiefs, on the cheerful bowl, yea, and on our vessels of various kinds, as well as upon our hearts? Why is all this, but because of the inseparable connexion between Wilkes and liberty; liberty that came down, if not fell, from heaven; whom all England and the world worshippeth?

Thoughts upon Liberty, 1772.

'THERE IS NO POWER BUT OF GOD'

'By power, I here mean supreme power, the power over life and death, and consequently over our liberty and property, and all things of an inferior nature.'

But have not the people, in every age and nation, the right of disposing of this power; of investing therewith whom they please, either one or more persons; and that, in what proportion they see good, and upon what conditions? Consequently, if those conditions are not observed, have they not a right to take away the power they gave? And does not this imply that they are the judges whether those conditions are observed or not? Otherwise, if the receivers were judges of their own cause, this right would fall into nothing.

To prove this, that the people in every country are the source of power, it is argued thus: 'All men living upon earth are naturally equal; none is above another; and all are naturally free, masters of their own actions. It manifestly follows, no man can have any power over another, unless by his own consent. The power therefore which the governors in any nation enjoy, must be originally derived from the people, and presupposes an original compact between them and their first governors.'

This seems to be the opinion which is now generally espoused by men of understanding and education; and that (if I do not mistake) not in England alone, but almost in every civilized nation. And it is usually espoused with the fullest and strongest persuasion, as a truth little less than self-evident, as what is clear beyond all possibility of doubt, what commands the assent of all reasonable men. Hence if any man affected to deny it, he would in most companies be rather hooted at than argued with; it being so absurd to oppose what is confirmed by the general suffrage of mankind.

The supposition, then, that the people are the origin of power, is in every way indefensible. It is absolute over-turned by the very principle on which it is supposed to stand; namely, that a right of choosing his Governors belongs to every partaker of human nature. If this be so, then it belongs to every individual of the human species; consequently, not to freeholders alone, but to all men; not to men only, but to women also; nor only to adult men and women, to those who have lived one-and-twenty years, but to those who have lived eighteen or twenty, as well as those who have lived threescore. But none did ever maintain this, nor probably ever will. Therefore this boasted principle falls to the ground, and the whole superstructure with it. So common sense brings us back to the grand truth, 'There is no power but of God'.

From Thoughts concerning the Origin of Power, 1772.

Chapter VIII

WESLEY AND WAR

Wesley loathed war in all its forms, but endorsed it in certain circumstances. In this he was no different from the majority of Christians. But it should be remembered that the problem of war in the eighteenth century did not press so overwhelmingly on the ordinary citizen as it does to-day. Armies were small, and often composed of foreign mercenaries. Christian reformers tended to be preoccupied with the abolition of slavery and other great social issues and in these matters, as described elsewhere in this book, Wesley took the progressive and unpopular side. With regard to war itself, he gave an account in his tract on *The Doctrine of Original Sin*, which ridicules its folly and exposes its wickedness. This amazing passage is printed below in full.

More than once Wesley protested against the operations of the press-gang, and readers will remember the inspiring story of John Nelson, one of Wesley's Lay Assistants, who was press-ganged, and made what must be the first Methodist profession of Christian pacifism, before he was released through the intervention of Wesley himself.

The Evil of War

But there is a still greater and more undeniable proof that the very foundations of all things, civil and religious, are utterly out of course in the Christian as well as the heathen world. There is a still more horrid reproach to the Christian name, yea, to the name of man, to all reason and humanity. There is war in the world! war between men! war between Christians! I mean, between those that bear the name of Christ, and profess to 'walk as he also walked'. Now, who can reconcile war, I will not say to religion, but to any degree of reason or common sense?

But is there not a cause? O yes: 'The causes of war', as the same writer observes, 'are innumerable. Some of the chief are these: The ambition of Princes, or the corruption of their Ministers: Difference of opinion; as: whether flesh be bread, or bread be flesh; whether the juice of the grape be blood or wine; what is the best colour for a coat, whether black, white or grey; and whether it should be long or short, whether narrow or wide. Nor are there any wars so furious as those occasioned by such difference of opinions.

'Sometimes two Princes make war to decide which of them shall dispossess a third of his dominions. Sometimes a war is commenced, because another Prince is too strong; sometimes, because he is too weak. Sometimes our neighbours want the things which we have, or have the things which we want: so both fight, until they take ours, or we take theirs. It is a reason for invading a country, if the people have been wasted by famine, destroyed by pestilence, or embroiled by faction, or to attack our nearest ally, if part of his land would make our dominions more round and compact.

'Another cause of making war is this: A crew are driven by a storm they know not where; at length they make the land and go ashore; they are entertained with kindness. They give the country a new name, set up a stone or rotten plank for a memorial; murder a dozen of the natives, and bring away a couple by force. Here commences a new right of dominion: ships are sent, and the natives driven out or destroyed. And this is done to civilize and convert a barbarous and idolatrous people.'

But, whatever be the cause, let us calmly and impartially consider the thing itself. Here are forty thousand men gathered together on this plain. What are they going to do? See, there are thirty or forty thousand more at a little distance. And these are going to shoot them through the head or body, to stab them or split their skulls, and send most of their souls into everlasting fire, as fast as possibly they can. Why so? What harm have they done to them? O none at all! They do not so much as know them. But a man, who is King of France, has a quarrel with another man, who is King of England. So these Frenchmen are to kill as many of these Englishmen as they can, to prove the King of France is in the right. Now, what an argument is this! What a method of proof! What an amazing way of deciding controversies! What must mankind be, before such a thing as war could ever be known or thought of upon earth? How shocking, how inconceivable a want must there have been of common understanding, as well as common humanity, before any two Governors, or any two nations in the universe, could once think of such a method of decision? If, then, all nations, Pagan, Mahometan, and Christian, do, in fact, make this their last resort, what further proof do we need of the utter degeneracy of all nations from the plainest principles of reason and virtue? of the absolute want, both of common sense and common humanity, which runs through the whole race of mankind?

In how just and strong a light is this placed by the writer cited before: 'I gave him a description of cannons, muskets, pistols, swords, bayonets; of sieges, attacks, mines, counter-mines, bombardments, of engagements by sea and land; ships sunk with a thousand men, twenty killed on each side, dying groans, limbs flying in the air; smoke, noise, trampling to death under horses' feet, flight, pursuit, victory; fields strewed with carcases, left for food to dogs and beasts of prey, and, further, of plundering, stripping, ravishing, burning and destroying. I assured him, I had seen a hundred enemies blown up at once in a siege, and as many in a ship, and beheld the dead bodies drop down in pieces from the clouds, to the great diversion of the spectators.'

Is it not astonishing, beyond all expression, that this is the naked truth? that, within a short term of years this has been the real case in almost every part of even the Christian world? And meanwhile we gravely talk of the 'dignity of our nature' in its present state! This is really surprising, and might easily drive even a well-tempered man to say, 'One might bear with men, if they would be content with those vices and follies to which nature has entitled them. I am not provoked at the sight of a pickpocket, a gamester, a politician, a suborner, a traitor or the like. This is all according to the natural course of things. But when I behold a lump of deformity and diseases, both in body and mind, smitten with pride, it breaks all the measures of my patience, neither shall I ever be able to comprehend how such an animal and such a vice can tally together'.

And surely all our declamations on the strength of human reason, and the eminence of our virtues, are no more than the cant and jargon of pride and ignorance, so long as there is such a thing as war in the world. Men in general can never be allowed to be reasonable creatures, till they know

not war any more. So long as this monster stalks un-
controlled, where is reason, virtue, humanity? They are
utterly excluded, they have no place, they are a name, and
nothing more. If even a Heathen were to give an account
of an age wherein reason and virtue reigned, he would
allow no war to have place therein. So Ovid of the Golden
age:

> *Nondum praecipites cingebant oppida fossae;*
> *Non galeae, non ensis erat. Sine militis usu*
> *Mollia securae peragebant otia gentes.*

> Steep ditches did not then the towns surround,
> Nor glittering helm, nor slaughtering sword was found;
> Nor arms had they to wield, nor wars to wage,
> But peace and safety crown'd the blissful age.

The Doctrine of Original Sin.

WESLEY'S RESPONSE TO A THREATENED INVASION OF
ENGLAND

SIR,

A few days since, Mr. Whitefield and I desired a friend to
ask your advice—to whom it would be proper to make an
offer of raising a company of volunteers for His Majesty's
service. We apprehended the number would be about five
hundred. Finding Mr. Whitefield has since been persuaded
that such an offer is premature, I am constrained to make
the following, independently of him: To raise, for His
Majesty's service, at least two hundred volunteers, to be
supported by contributions among themselves; and to be
ready, in case of invasion, to act for a year, if needed so
long, at His Majesty's pleasure; only within . . . miles
of London.

If this be acceptable to His Majesty, they beg to have
arms out of the Tower, giving the usual security for their
return; and some of His Majesty's sergeants to instruct
them in the military exercise.

I am now hastening to Bristol, on account of the election;
but if my return to London would be of any service, you
may command, Sir, your obedient servant.

Letter to the Hon. James West, March 1, 1756.

GOD OUR DEFENCE

DEAR SAMMY,

The alarm has been general in England as well as Ireland, particularly in the maritime parts. But it has done abundantly more good than harm to the work of God. The children of God have been greatly stirred up and have been more instant in prayer. And many men of the world have been greatly awakened, and continued so to this day. Most of those who have the fullest intercourse with God believe our enemies will never be permitted to land in England. And, indeed, God has already given abundant proof of His hearing prayer: first, in their not landing at Plymouth, where they stayed gaping and staring for eight-and forty hours while they might with all ease have destroyed both the dock and the town; secondly, in the malignant fever which has broken out in their fleet, and already destroyed several thousands of men.

Letter to Samuel Bradburn, October 10, 1779.

CHAPTER IX

THE AMERICAN WAR OF INDEPENDENCE

'IT is amazing', says Dr. Maldwyn Edwards, 'that nobody has thought of dealing fully with Wesley's part in the War of American Independence. No layman was so prominent, nor had so great an influence.' Why should Wesley have been so deeply interested in the question? First, he had memories of the colonies. Second, in 1769 the first Methodist preachers had been sent to America, followed in 1771 by Francis Asbury. America was on Wesley's horizon for the preaching of the Gospel. Third, he had a horror of the fratricidal strife and fourth, while at the beginning, as his famous letter to Lord Dartmouth shows, he had undoubted sympathies with the Colonists, as the struggle proceeded his loyalist convictions were aroused and he became their antagonist.

Wesley's concern and the change in attitude may be traced through the succession of letters and pamphlets he wrote, from the letter to Lord Dartmouth already alluded to, to the *Calm Address to our American Colonies* 1775, his more pacific *Seasonable Address to Inhabitants of Great Britain* 1776, his truculent reply to Dr. Price in *Some Observations on Liberty* 1776, with his *Calm Address to Inhabitants of England* 1777.

Some may question the value of including Wesley's judgements on the War of Independence in these Selections. Yet they could hardly be excluded, since they are necessary to a complete picture of Wesley as Christian citizen and pamphleteer, and they are instructive again as showing how in the world of affairs the judgement of the Christian is likely to be tested and may be at fault.

METHODISM GOES TO AMERICA

Question 13:—We have a pressing call from our brethren at New York (who have built a preaching-house), to come over and help them. Who is willing to go?

Answer:—Richard Boardman and Joseph Pilmoor.

Question 14:—What can we do further in token of our brotherly love?

Answer:—Let us now make a collection among ourselves. This was immediately done, and out of it £50 were allotted towards the payment of the debt, and about £20 given to our brethren for their passage.

Minutes of Leeds Conference, 1769.

FRANCIS ASBURY

Our brethren in America call aloud for help; who are willing to go over and help them?

Minutes of Bristol Conference, 1771.

I spoke my mind, and made an offer of myself. It was accepted by Mr. John Wesley and others, who judged I had a call.   FRANCIS ASBURY: *Journal, August*, 1771.

I LET YOU LOOSE ON THE GREAT CONTINENT OF AMERICA

I let you loose, George, on the great Continent of America. Publish your message in the open face of the sun, and do all the good you can.

I am, dear George, yours affectionately,

JOHN WESLEY.

Letter to George Shadford, March, 1773.

FIRST THOUGHTS ON THE CONFLICT

(*The Earl of Dartmouth who received the following letter was Secretary of State for the Colonies in* 1722 *and Lord Privy Seal,* 1775–82. *Lord North to whom a similar letter was sent, was Prime Minister. The Battle of Bunker's Hill was fought June* 17, 1775.)

In the way to Dublin, June 14, 1775.

MY LORD,

I would not speak, as it may seem to be concerning myself with things that lie out of my province. But I dare not refrain from it any longer; I think silence in the present case would be a sin against God, against my country, and against my own soul.

All my prejudices are against the Americans. For I am an High Churchman, the son of an High Churchman, bred up from my childhood in the highest notions of passive obedience and non-resistance. And yet, in spite of all my rooted prejudice, I cannot avoid thinking (if I think at all) that an oppressed people asked for nothing more than their legal rights, and that in the most modest and inoffensive manner which the nature of the thing would allow.

But waiving this, waiving all considerations of right and wrong, I ask, Is it common sense to use force toward the Americans? A letter now before me says, 'Four hundred of the Regulars and forty of the Militia were killed in the last skirmish'. What a disproportion! And this is the first essay of raw men against regular troops!

You see, my Lord, whatever has been affirmed, these men will not be frightened. And it seems they will not be conquered so easily as was at first imagined. They will probably dispute every inch of ground, and, if they die, die sword in hand.

Indeed, some of our valiant officers say, 'Two thousand men will not clear America of these rebels'. No, nor twenty thousand, nor perhaps treble that number, be they rebels or not. They are as strong men as you; they are as valiant as you, if not abundantly more valiant. For they are one and all enthusiasts—enthusiasts for liberty. They are calm deliberate enthusiasts. And we know how this principle

> Breathes into softest souls stern love of war,
> And thirst of vengeance, and contempt of death.

We know men animated with this will leap into a fire or rush upon a cannon's mouth.

'But they have no experience of war.' And how much more have our troops? How few of them ever saw a battle? 'But they have no discipline.' That is an entire mistake. Already they have near as much as our army. And they will learn more of it every day. So that in a short time they will understand it as well as their assailants.

'But they are divided among themselves: so you are informed by various letters and memorials.' So, I doubt not, was poor Rehoboam informed concerning the ten tribes! So (nearer our times) was Philip informed concerning the people of the Netherlands! No, my Lord, they are terribly united; not in the Province of New England only, but down as low as the Jerseys and Pennsylvania the bulk of the people are so united that to speak a word in favour of the present English measures would almost endanger a man's life. Those who inform me of this (one of whom was with me last week, lately come from Philadelphia) are no sycophants; they say nothing to curry favour; they have nothing to gain or lose by me. But they speak with sorrow of heart what they have seen with their eyes and heard with their own ears.

Those men think one and all, be it right or wrong, that they are contending *pro aris et focis*, for their wives, children, liberty! What advantage have they herein over men that fight only for pay! none of whom care a straw for the cause wherein they are engaged, most of whom strongly disapprove of it.

But, my Lord, this is not all. We have thousands of enemies, perhaps more dangerous than French or Spaniards. They are landed already; they fill our cities, our towns, our villages. As I travel four or five thousand miles every year, I have an opportunity of conversing freely with more persons of every denomination than any one else in the three kingdoms. I cannot therefore but know the general disposition of the people, English, Scots, and Irish; and I know an huge majority of them are exasperated almost to madness. Exactly so they were throughout England and Scotland about the year 1640; and in great measure by the same means—by inflammatory papers, which were spread, as they are now, with the utmost diligence in every corner of the land. Hereby the bulk of the people were effectually cured of all love and reverence for the King; so that, first despising, then hating him, they were just ripe for open rebellion. And I assure your Lordship so they are now: they want nothing but a leader.

Two circumstances more deserve to be considered: the one that there was at that time a general decay of trade almost throughout the kingdom; the other that there was an uncommon dearness of provisions. The case is the same in both respects at this day. So that even now there are multitudes of people that, having nothing to do and nothing to eat, are ready for the first bidder; and that, without inquiring into the merits of the cause, would flock to any that would give them bread.

Upon the whole I am really sometimes afraid that 'this evil is of the Lord'. When I consider (to say nothing of ten thousand other vices shocking to human nature) the astonishing *luxury* of the rich and the *profaneness* of rich and poor, I doubt whether general dissoluteness of manners does not de-

mand a general visitation. Perhaps the decree is already gone
forth from the Governor of the world. Perhaps even now,

> As he that buys surveys a ground,
> So the destroying angel measures it around.
> Calm he surveys the perishing nation,
> Ruin behind him stalks and empty desolation.

But we Englishmen are too wise to acknowledge that God
has anything to do in the world! Otherwise should we not
seek Him by fasting and prayer before He lets the lifted
thunder drop? O my Lord, if your Lordship can do anything let it not be wanting! For God's sake, for the sake of
the King, of the nation, of your lovely family, remember
Rehoboam! Remember Philip the Second! Remember
King Charles the First!

I am, with true regard, my Lord,

Your Lordship's obedient servant.

Letter to the Earl of Dartmouth, June 14, 1775.

A CHANGE OF VIEW

I was of a different judgement on this head, till I read a
tract entitled, *Taxation no Tyranny*.[1] But as soon as I
received more light myself, I judged it my duty to impart
it to others. I therefore extracted the chief arguments from
that treatise, and added an application to those whom it
most concerns. I was well aware of the treatment this
would bring upon myself; but let it be, so I may in any
degree serve my King and country.

A late tract wrote in answer to this, is wrote in just such
a spirit as I expected. The writer asserts twenty times, 'He
that is taxed without his own consent, that is, without
being represented, is a slave'. I answer, No; I have no
representative in Parliament; but I am taxed, yet I am no
slave. Yea, nine in ten throughout England have no representative, no vote; yet they are no slaves; they enjoy both
civil and religious liberty to the utmost extent.

He replies, 'But they may have votes if they will; they
may have purchased freeholds'. What! Can every man in
England purchase a freehold? No, not one in an hundred.
But, be that as it may, they have no vote now; yet they are
no slaves, they are the freest men in the world.

[1] Written by Dr. Samuel Johnson.

the contrary. I contributed my mite toward putting out the flame which rages all over the land. This I have more opportunity of observing than any other man in England. I see with pain to what a height this already rises, in every part of the nation, and I see many pouring oil into the flame, by crying out, 'How unjustly, how cruelly the King is using the poor Americans, who are only contending for their liberty, and for their legal privileges!'

Now there is no possible way to put out this flame, or hinder its rising higher and higher, but to show that the Americans are not used either cruelly or unjustly, that they are not injured at all, seeing they are not contending for liberty (this they had even in its full extent, both civil and religious); neither for any legal privileges, for they enjoy all that charters grant: but what they contend for is, the illegal privilege of being exempt from parliamentary taxation. A privilege this, which no charter ever gave to any American colony yet; which no charter can give unless it be confirmed both by King, Lords, and Commons, which in fact, our Colonies never had, which they never claimed till the present reign, and probably they would not have claimed it now, had they not been incited thereto by letters from England. One of these was read, according to the desire of the writer, not only at the Continental Congress, but likewise in many congregations throughout the combined provinces. It advised them, To seize upon all the King's officers, and exhorted them, 'stand valiantly, only for six months, and in that time there will be such commotions in England that you may have your own terms'.

This being the real state of the question, without any colouring or aggravation, what impartial man can either blame the King, or commend the Americans?

With this view, to quench the fire, by laying the blame where it was due, the *Calm Address* was written.

Letter in ' Lloyd's Evening Post,' Journal,
Monday, November 27, 1775.

THE HORRORS OF FRATRICIDAL STRIFE

The great danger of which, as well as the cause of this unparalleled and fatal strife, I would beg leave to present to your view in a piece of fine painting, done by an abler master; 'See! Here are some thousands of our brave countrymen gathered together on this plain; they are followed by the most tender and feeling emotions of wives, children, and an innumerable multitude of their thoughtful, humane, and sympathizing countrymen. Then turn your eyes and behold a superior number at a little distance, of their brethren, "flesh of their flesh, and bone of their bone", who only a few years since emigrated to the dreary wilds of America. These also are followed with the most tender feelings of wives, children, and countrymen. See, they advance towards each other, well prepared with every instrument of death! But what are they going to do? To shoot each other through the head or heart; to stab and butcher each other, and hasten (it is to be feared) one another into the everlasting burnings. Why so? What harm have they done to one another? Why, none at all. Most of them are entire strangers to each other. But a matter is in dispute relative to the mode of taxation. So these countrymen, children of the same parents, are to murder each other with all possible haste, to prove who is in the right. Now, what an argument is this! What a method of proof! What an amazing way of deciding controversies! But so it is; and O what horrors attend it! At what a price is the decision made! By the blood and wounds of thousands; the burning cities, ravaging and laying waste the country.' Now, who that seriously considers this awful contest, can help lamenting the astonishing want of wisdom in our brethren to decide the matter without bloodshed? What, are there no wise men among us? none that are able to judge between brethren? But brother goeth to war against brother; and that in the very sight of the Heathen. Surely this is a sore evil among us. O how are the mighty fallen! How is wisdom perished from the wise! What a flood of folly and madness has broke in upon us!

Seasonable Address to the Inhabitants of Great Britain, 1776.

STILL TRYING TO QUENCH THE FIRE

On Thursday I wrote *A Calm Address to the Inhabitants of England*. May God bless this, as he did the former, to the quenching of that evil fire which is still among us!

Journal, Thursday, February 6, 1777.

THE NEW APPEAL

About a year and a half ago, being exceedingly pained at what I saw or heard continually, I wrote a little tract entitled, *A Calm Address to our American Colonies;* but the ports being just then shut up by the Americans, I could not send it abroad, as I designed. However, it was not lost; within a few months, fifty, or perhaps an hundred thousand copies, in newspapers and otherwise, were dispersed throughout Great Britain and Ireland. The effect exceeded my most sanguine hopes. The eyes of many people were opened; they saw things in quite a different light. They perceived, and that with the utmost clearness, how they had been hoodwinked before. They found they had been led unawares into all the wilds of political enthusiasm, as far distant from truth and common sense as from the real love of their country.

I am encouraged hereby to address myself once more, not indeed to my countrymen afar off, but to you who remain in your native land, who are inhabitants of old England. I have no private views in doing this. I attend no great man's table. I have nothing to ask, either of the King, or any of his Ministers. You may easily believe this; for if I had sought wealth or preferment half a century ago, I should hardly think it worth while to seek it now, when I have one foot in the grave. But I have a view to contribute all that in me lies to the public welfare and tranquillity. A flame was studiously kindled some time since, which threatened to involve the whole nation. By the blessing of God, it is greatly checked; it does not spread, or blaze as formerly. But it is not quite put out. I wish to quench the remains of that evil fire.

My view is, as far as is possible, to lessen, if not remove, the misunderstandings under which many honest, well-meaning men are labouring to this day; misunderstandings which have caused much animosity, nay, much bitterness and rancour in their minds against those who equally 'strive to have a conscience void of offence towards God and towards man'. I would fain have all these duly sensible of the blessings which they enjoy; that they may be thankful to the Giver of every blessing, and may love one another as He has loved us.

Surely every man of candour and humanity must wish well to such an attempt; in the prosecution of which I will

first endeavour to set down, in as plain and artless a manner
as I can, according to the best light I have, the real state
of those affairs which have occasioned these misunderstandings; and then add two or three short reflections, which I
conceive naturally deducible therefrom.

A Calm Address to the Inhabitants of England, 1777.

A WORD TO METHODISTS

Permit me to add a few more words to you, a small part of
whom dissent from, but the far greater part remain in, the
Church; you who are vulgarly called Methodists. Do any
of you blaspheme God or the King? None of you, I trust,
who are in connexion with me. I would no more continue
in fellowship with those who continued in such a practice,
than with whoremongers, or sabbath-breakers, or thieves,
or drunkards, or common swearers. But there are not a
few who go under that name, though they have no
connexion with us; yea, though they cordially hate us as
dreadful heretics, for believing that 'God willeth all men
to be saved'; who hate the King and all his Ministers only
less than they do an Arminian; and who speak all manner
of evil of them in private, if not in public too. But suffer
me to ask, Is this well done? Is it gratitude? Is it prudence?
In the name of wonder, what could His Majesty have done
for you which he has not done? What would you have?
Can you tell? What can you desire more than you have
already? Have you not full liberty of conscience in every
respect, without any shadow of restraint? In what other
nation under the sun is such religious liberty to be found?
Have you not full liberty, with regard to your life, to your
person, and to your goods? In what other country upon
earth is such civil liberty to be found? If you are not
thankful to God and the King for these blessings, you are
utterly unworthy of them. Is it prudence to speak in so
bitter and contemptuous a manner of such Governors as
God has given you? What, if by the bitterness of your
spirit, the acrimony of your language, and the inflammatory
libels which you spread abroad, you could carry your point,
unhinge the present Government, and set up another in its
stead! what would you gain thereby? Would another
Government allow you more liberty than you now enjoy?

Could they give you a more unbounded liberty of conscience? It is impossible! Would they give you a larger measure of civil liberty? They could not if they would. And certainly they would not give you the liberty of railing at your Governors, and stirring up your fellow-subjects against them. If you did this, you would not only lose your goods, but probably your life also. On the other hand, what if the present Government should continue in spite of all your disloyal practices! have you any assurance, have you any reason to believe, that our Governors will always be so patient? Nay, undoubtedly, when things of greater moment are settled, they will find a time for you. Your present behaviour will then be remembered; perhaps not altogether to your advantage. It is not the ignorance but the wisdom of your Governors which occasions their present silence. And if you go on thus, be assured, sooner or later, you will meet with your reward. There is no need that the King should do anything; He needs only not to restrain; that is enough. There are those on every side who are now ready to swallow you up. You will then wish you had been wise in time, when your wisdom comes too late; when the King of kings 'laughs at your calamity, and mocks while your fear cometh'.

A Calm Address to the Inhabitants of England, 1777.

The True Note of Reconciliation

My Dear Brethren,

You were never in your lives in so critical a situation as you are at this time. It is your part to be peace-makers, to be loving and tender to all, but to addict yourselves to no party. In spite of all situations, of rough or smooth words, say not one word against one or the other side. Keep yourselves pure, do all you can to help and soften all, but beware how you adopt another's jar.

See that you act in full union with each other, this is of the utmost consequence. Not only let there be no bitterness or anger but no shyness or coldness between you. Mark all them that would set one of you against the other. Some such will never be wanting. But give them no countenance, rather ferret them out and drag them into open day. . . .

A Line to all the preachers in America, enclosed in a letter to Thomas Rankin, March 1, 1775.

Chapter X

WESLEY AND SLAVERY

O<small>NE</small> great achievement of the eighteenth century was the
movement for the Abolition of the Slave Trade, in which the
names of Granville Sharpe, Thomas Clarkson and William
Wilberforce figure so largely. It is sometimes overlooked that
to the awakening of public opinion on the subject Wesley
brought his own powers of advocacy. Interested in negroes
from his Georgia days, and, plied with information from Virginia,
his concern was kindled to flame by reading the attacks on the
Slave Trade written by Antony Benzet, the Quaker referred to
in the *Journal* under date February 12, 1772. Wesley's *Thoughts
upon Slavery*, 1774 was the direct outcome. From the start of the
agitation for the abolition of the Slave Trade he was consulted
by Clarkson, and that his concern continued unabated is shown
by the Sermon on Slavery preached at Bristol, described in the
Journal under date, Monday, March 3, 1788, when he was eighty-
five, and by the still more famous letter to Wilberforce in the year
he died. How unabated his interest was, is shown by the fact that
this letter was inspired by the reading two days before of yet
another book on slavery, the life of a negro slave, Gustavus
Vasa. To this he refers in the letter.

One qualification should be kept in mind in reading the extracts from *Thoughts upon Slavery*. The vivid account of the African
peoples from whom the unhappy victims of the slave trade were
derived, is perhaps a little unduly tinged with a conception of
the virtues of primitive peoples to which an age which idealized
the state of nature was prone. In this, Wesley was too receptive
a reader of Benzet.

CONCERN FOR SLAVES IN AMERICA

I came to Mr. Belinger's plantation, where the rain kept
me till Friday. Here I met an old negro who was tolerably
well instructed in the principles of Christianity, and who,
as well as his fellow negroes and a half Indian woman
(one that had an Indian mother and a Spanish father)
seemed earnestly desirous of further instruction. One of
them said, 'When I was at Ashley-Ferry, I could go to
church every Sunday; but here we are buried in the

woods.   Though if there was any church within five or six miles, I am so lame I cannot walk, but I would crawl thither'.

Mr. Belinger sent a negro lad with me on Friday, who conducted me safe to Purrysburg.

This lad too I found both very desirous and very capable of instruction. And perhaps one of the easiest and shortest ways to instruct the American negroes in Christianity, would be, first, to inquire after and find out some of the most serious of the planters. Then, having inquired of them which of their slaves were best inclined and understood English, to go to them from plantation to plantation, staying as long as appeared necessary at each. Three or four gentlemen in Carolina I have been with that would be sincerely glad of such an assistant, who might pursue his work with no more hindrances than must everywhere attend the preaching of the Gospel.

Journal, Wednesday, April 30, 1737.

TEACHING CHRIST TO A NEGRO LAD ON THE WAY HOME

I began instructing a negro lad in the principles of Christianity.

Journal, Monday, December 26, 1737.

LETTERS FROM VIRGINIA

I was much affected about this time, by a letter sent from a gentleman in Virginia. Part of it runs thus:
'The poor negro slaves here never heard of Jesus, or his religion, till they arrived at the land of their slavery in America; whom their masters generally neglect, as though immortality was not the privilege of their souls, in common with their own. These poor Africans are the principal objects of my compassion, and, I think, the most proper subject of your charity.'

Journal, Sunday, July 27, 1755.

There are thousands of negroes in this colony who still continue in the grossest ignorance, and are as rank Pagans as they were in the wilds of Africa. Not a few of these are within the bounds of my congregation. But all are not of this character. Upon some my ministry of late has been successful. Two Sundays ago I had the pleasure of seeing forty of their black faces at the Lord's Table, several of whom give unusual evidence of their sincerity in religion. Last Sunday I baptized seven or eight, who had been catechized for some time. Indeed many of them appear determined to press into the kingdom, and I am persuaded will find an abundant entrance when many of the children of the kingdom are shut out.

Journal, Monday, March 1, 1756.
Quotation from a letter from the Rev. Mr. Davies in Virginia.

PREACHING TO SLAVES

I preached at Wandsworth. A gentleman come from America has again opened a door in the desolate place. In the morning I preached in Mr. Gilbert's house. Two negro servants of his, and a mulatto, appear to be much awakened. Shall not his saving health be made know to all nations?

Journal, Tuesday, January 17, 1758.

I rode to Wandsworth, and baptized two negroes belonging to Mr. Gilbert, a gentleman lately come from Antigua. One of these is deeply convinced of sin; the other rejoices in God her Saviour, and is the first African Christian I have known. But shall not our Lord, in due time, have these Heathens also 'for his inheritance?'

Journal, Wednesday, November, 29, 1758.

(Out of this association with Gilbert came the beginning of Methodist Missions in the West Indies, the first ever undertaken by Methodists.)

A QUAKER'S BOOK ON THE SLAVE TRADE

In returning, I read a very different book, published by an honest Quaker, on that execrable sum of all villanies, commonly called the Slave-trade. I read of nothing like it in the heathen world, whether ancient or modern. And it infinitely exceeds, in every instance of barbarity, whatever Christian slaves suffer in Mahometan countries.

Journal, Wednesday, February 12, 1772.

DESCRIPTION OF AN AFRICAN PEOPLE

The natives of the kingdom of Benin are a reasonable and good-natured people. They are sincere and inoffensive, and do no injustice either to one another or to strangers. They are eminently civil and courteous: If you make them a present, they endeavour to repay it double: and if they are trusted till the ship returns the next year, they are sure honestly to pay the whole debt. Theft is punished among them, although not with the same severity as murder. If a man and woman of any quality are taken in adultery, they are certain to be put to death, and their bodies thrown on a dunghill, and left a prey to wild beasts. They are punctually just and honest in their dealings; and are also very charitable, the King and the great Lords taking care to employ all that are capable of any work. And those that are utterly helpless they keep for God's sake; so that here also are no beggars. The inhabitants of Congo and Angola are generally a quiet people. They discover a good understanding, and behave in a friendly manner to strangers, being of a mild temper and an affable carriage. Upon the whole, therefore, the Negroes who inhabit the coast of Africa, from the river Senegal to the southern bounds of Angola, are so far from being the stupid, senseless, brutish, lazy barbarians, the fierce, cruel, perfidious savages they have been described, that, on the contrary, they are represented, by them who have no motive to flatter them, as remarkably sensible, considering the few advantages they have for improving their understanding; as industrious to the highest degree, perhaps more so than any other natives of so warm a climate; as fair, just, and honest in all their dealings, unless where white men have taught them to be otherwise; and as far more mild, friendly, and kind to strangers than any of our forefathers were. Our forefathers! Where shall we find at this day, among the fair-faced natives of Europe, a nation generally practising the justice, mercy, and truth, which are found among these poor Africans?

Thoughts upon Slavery, 1774.

THE CAPTURE OF SLAVES

In what manner are they procured? Part of them by fraud. Captains of ships, from time to time, have invited

Negroes to come on board, and then carried them away. But far more have been procured by force. The Christians, landing upon their coasts, seized as many as they found, men, women, and children, and transported them to America. It was about 1551 that the English began trading to Guinea; at first, for gold and elephants' teeth, but soon after, for men. In 1556, Sir John Hawkins sailed with two ships to Cape Verd, where he sent eighty men on shore to catch Negroes. But the natives flying, they fell farther down, and there set the men on shore, 'to burn their town and take the inhabitants'. But they met with such resistance that they had seven men killed, and took but ten Negroes. So they went still farther down, till, having taken enough, they proceeded to the West Indies and sold them.

It was some time before the Europeans found a more compendious way of procuring African slaves, by prevailing upon them to make war upon each other, and to sell their prisoners. Till then they seldom had any wars; but were in general quiet and peaceable. But the white men first taught them drunkenness and avarice, and then hired them to sell one another. Nay, by this means, even their Kings are induced to sell their own subjects. So Mr. Moore, factor of the African Company in 1730, informs us: 'When the King of Barsalli wants goods or brandy, he sends to the English Governor at James's Fort, who immediately sends a sloop. Against the time it arrives, he plunders some of his neighbours' towns, selling the people for the goods he wants. At other times he falls upon one of his own towns, and makes bold to sell his own subjects.' So Monsieur Brue says, 'I wrote to the King' (not the same), 'if he had a sufficient number of slaves, I would treat with him. He seized three hundred of his own people, and sent word he was ready to deliver them for the goods'. He adds: 'Some of the natives are always ready' (when well paid) 'to surprise and carry off their own countrymen. They come at night without noise, and if they find any lone cottage, surround it and carry off all the people.' Barbot, another French factor, says, 'Many of the slaves sold by the Negroes are prisoners of war, or taken in the incursions they make into their enemies' territories. Others are stolen. Abundance of little Blacks, of both sexes, are stolen away by their neighbours, when found abroad on the road, or in the woods, or else in the corn-fields, at the time of year when their parents keep them there all day to scare away the devouring birds '.   That their own parents sell them is utterly false: Whites, not Blacks, are without natural affection!

Thoughts upon Slavery, 1774.

THE TRAFFIC ACROSS THE SEA

Thus they are procured.   But in what numbers and in what manner are they carried to America?   Mr. Anderson, in his *History of Trade and Commerce*, observes: 'England supplies her American Colonies with Negro slaves, amounting in number to about an hundred thousand every year': that is, so many are taken on board our ships; but at least ten thousand of them die in the voyage; about a fourth part more die at the different islands, in what is called the seasoning.   So that at an average, in the passage and seasoning together, thirty thousand die; that is, properly, are murdered.   O Earth, O Sea, cover not thou their blood!

When they are brought down to the shore in order to be sold, our Surgeons thoroughly examine them, and that quite naked, women and men, without any distinction; those that are approved are set on one side.   In the meantime, a burning iron, with the arms or name of the company, lies in the fire, with which they are marked on the breast.   Before they are put into the ships, their masters strip them of all they have on their backs; so that they come on board stark naked, women as well as men.   It is common for several hundred of them to be put on board one vessel, where they are stowed together in as little room as it is possible for them to be crowded.   It is easy to suppose what a condition they must soon be in, between heat, thirst, and stench of various kinds.   So that it is no wonder so many should die in the passage; but rather, that any survive it.

When the vessels arrive at their destined port, the Negroes are again exposed naked to the eyes of all that flock together, and the examination of their purchasers.   Then they are separated to the plantations of their several masters, to see each other no more.   Here you may see mothers hanging over their daughters, bedewing their naked breasts with tears, and daughters clinging to their parents, till the whipper soon obliges them to part.   And what can be more wretched than the condition they enter upon? Banished from their country, from their friends and relations for ever, from every comfort of life, they are reduced to a state scarce anyway preferable to that of beasts of burden. In general, a few roots, not of the nicest kind, usually yams or potatoes, are their food; and two rags, that neither screen them from the heat of the day, nor the cold of the night, their covering. Their sleep is very short, their labour continual, and frequently above their strength; so that death sets many of them at liberty before they have lived out half their days. The time they work in the West Indies, is from daybreak to noon, and from two o'clock till dark; during which time, they are attended by overseers, who, if they think them dilatory, or think anything not so well done as it should be, whip them most unmercifully, so that you may see their bodies long after wealed and scarred usually from the shoulders to the waist. And before they are suffered to go to their quarters, they have commonly something to do, as collecting herbage for the horses, or gathering fuel for the boilers; so that it is often past twelve before they can get home. Hence, if their food is not prepared, they are sometimes called to labour again, before they can satisfy their hunger. And no excuse will avail. If they are not in the field immediately, they must expect to feel the lash. Did the Creator intend that the noblest creatures in the visible world should live such a life as this?

Thoughts upon Slavery, 1774.

VILLANY NEVER NECESSARY

But if this manner of procuring and treating Negroes is not consistent either with mercy or justice, yet there is a plea for it which every man of business will acknowledge to be quite sufficient. Fifty years ago, one meeting an eminent Statesman in the lobby of the House of Commons, said, 'You have been long talking about justice and equity. Pray which is this Bill; equity or justice?' He answered very short and plain, 'D——n justice; it is necessity'. Here also the slave-holder fixes his foot; here he rests the strength of his cause. 'If it is not quite right, yet it must be so; there is an absolute necessity for it. It is necessary we should procure slaves; and when we have procured them, it is necessary to use them with severity, considering their stupidity, stubborness, and wickedness.'

I answer, you stumble at the threshold; I deny that villany is ever necessary. It is impossible that it should ever be necessary for any reasonable creature to violate all the laws of justice, mercy, and truth. No circumstances can make it necessary for a man to burst in sunder all the ties of humanity. It can never be necessary for a rational being to sink himself below a brute. A man can be under no necessity of degrading himself into a wolf. The absurdity of the supposition is so glaring that one would wonder any one can help seeing it.

This in general. But, to be more particular, I ask, First, What is necessary? and, Secondly, To what end? It may be answered, 'The whole method now used by the original purchasers of Negroes is necessary to the furnishing our colonies yearly with a hundred thousand slaves'. I grant this is necessary to that end. But how is that end necessary? How will you prove it necessary that one hundred, that one, of those slaves should be procured? 'Why, it is necessary to my gaining an hundred thousand pounds.' Perhaps so. But how is this necessary? It is very possible you might be both a better and a happier man if you had not a quarter of it. I deny that your gaining one thousand is necessary either to your present or eternal happiness. 'But, however, you must allow, these slaves are necessary for the cultivation of our islands; inasmuch as white men are not able to labour in hot climates.' I answer, First, It were better that all those islands should remain uncultivated for ever; yea, it were more desirable that they were altogether sunk in the depth of the sea, than that they should be cultivated at so high a price as the violation of justice, mercy, and truth. But, Secondly, the supposition on which you ground your argument is false. For white men, even Englishmen, are well able to labour in hot climates; provided they are temperate both in meat and drink, and that they inure themselves to it by degrees. I speak no more than I know by experience. It appears from the thermometer, that the summer heat in Georgia is frequently equal to that in Barbadoes, yea, to that under the line. And yet I and my family (eight in number) did employ all our spare time there, in felling of trees and clearing of ground, as hard labour as any Negro need be employed in. The German family, likewise, forty in number, were employed in all manner of labour. And this was so far from impairing our health, that we all continued perfectly well, while the idle ones round about us were swept away with a pestilence It is not true, therefore, that white men are not able to labour, even in hot climates, full as well as black. But if they were not it would be better that none should labour there, that the work should be left undone, than that myriads of innocent men should be murdered, and myriads more dragged into the basest slavery.

'But the furnishing us with slaves is necessary for the trade, and wealth, and glory of our nation.' Here are several mistakes. For, First, wealth is not necessary to the glory of any nation; but wisdom, virtue, justice, mercy, generosity, public spirit, love of our country. These are necessary to the real glory of a nation; but abundance of wealth is not. Men of understanding allow that the glory of England was full as high in Queen Elizabeth's time as it is now; although our riches and trade were then as much smaller, as our virtue was greater. But, Secondly, it is not clear that we should have either less money or trade (only less of that detestable trade of man-stealing), if there was not a Negro in all our islands, or in all English America. It is demonstrable, white men, inured to it by degrees, can work as well as them; and they would do it, were Negroes out of the way, and proper encouragement given them. However, Thirdly, I come back to the same point: Better no trade, than trade procured by villany. It is far better to have no wealth, than to gain wealth at the expense of virtue. Better is honest poverty, than all the riches bought by the tears, and sweat, and blood, of our fellow-creatures.

'However this be, it is necessary, when we have slaves, to use them with severity.' What, to whip them for every petty offence, till they are all in gore blood? to take that opportunity of rubbing pepper and salt into their raw flesh? to drop burning sealing-wax upon their skin? to castrate them? to cut off half their foot with an axe? to hang them on gibbets, that they may die by inches, with heat, and hunger, and thirst? to pin them down to the ground and then burn them by degrees, from the feet to

highway. You know they are procured by a deliberate series of more complicated villany (of fraud, robbery, and murder) than was ever practised either by Mahometans or Pagans; in particular, by murders, of all kinds; by the blood of the innocent poured upon the ground like water. Now, it is your money that pays the merchant, and through him the captain and the African butchers. You therefore are guilty, yea, principally guilty, of all these frauds, robberies, and murders. You are the spring that puts all the rest in motion; they would not stir a step without you; therefore, the blood of all these wretches who die before their time, whether in their country or elsewhere, lies upon your head. 'The blood of thy brother' (for, whether thou wilt believe it or no, such he is in the sight of Him that made him) 'crieth against thee from the earth,' from the ship, and from the waters. O, whatever it costs, put a stop to its cry before it be too late. Instantly, at any price, were it the half of your goods, deliver thyself from blood-guiltiness! Thy hands, thy bed, thy furniture, thy house, thy lands, are at present stained with blood. Surely it is enough; accumulate no more guilt; spill no more the blood of the innocent! Do not hire another to shed blood; do not pay him for doing it! Whether you are a Christian or no, show yourself a man! Be not more savage than a lion or a bear!

Thoughts upon Slavery, 1774.

A Prayer to God for Slaves

O thou God of love, thou who art loving to every man, and whose mercy is over all thy works; thou who art the Father of the spirits of all flesh, and who art rich in mercy unto all; thou who hast mingled of one blood all the nations upon earth; have compassion upon these outcasts of men, who are trodden down as dung upon the earth! Arise, and help these that have no helper, whose blood is spilt upon the ground like water! Are not these also the work of thine own hands, the purchase of thy Son's blood? Stir them up to cry unto thee in the land of their captivity; and let their complaint come up before thee; let it enter into thy ears! Make even those that lead them away captive to pity them, and turn their captivity as the rivers in the south. O burst thou all their chains in sunder; more especially the chains of their sins! Thou Saviour of all, make them free, that they may be free indeed!

Thoughts upon Slavery, 1774.

A Sermon on Slavery

I went on to Bristol, and having two or three quiet days, finished my sermon upon Conscience.

On Tuesday I gave notice of my design to preach on Thursday evening, upon (what is now the general topic) Slavery. In consequence of this, on Thursday, the house, from end to end, was filled with high and low, rich and poor. I preached on that ancient prophecy, 'God shall enlarge Japhet. And he shall dwell in the tents of Shem; and Canaan shall be his servant'. About the middle of the discourse, while there was on every side attention as night, a vehement noise arose, none could tell why, and shot like lightning through the whole congregation. The terror and confusion were inexpressible. You might have imagined it was a city taken by storm. The people rushed upon each other with the utmost violence, the benches were broken in pieces; and nine-tenths of the congregation appeared to be struck with the same panic. In about six minutes the storm ceased, almost as suddenly as it rose, and all being calm, I went on without the least interruption.

It was the strangest incident of the kind I ever remember; and believe none can account for it, without supposing some preternatural influence. Satan fought lest his kingdom should be delivered up. We set Friday apart as a day of fasting and prayer that God would remember those poor outcasts of men, and (what seems impossible with men, considering the wealth and power of their oppressors) make a way for them to escape, and break their chains in sunder.

Journal, Monday, March 3, 1788. (*Wesley is* 85.)

Wesley Writes to the Papers

Gentlemen,

I can easily believe what your correspondent affirms (*Review*, October, 1774), that there are some slave-holders who have a little humanity left, and that the Georgian laws

H

sell the blood of one slave only to each master, and prescribe the instruments wherewith he is to torture the rest.

What is still the general spirit of American slave-holders is observed in a letter from Philadelphia now before me.

As a farther influence of the inhumanity with which the poor negroes are treated, I will add two advertisements published in the public papers, one of Virginia, the other of North Carolina:

From the *Williamsburg Gazette*.

'Run away on the 10th inst., a lusty negro, named Bob ——. The said fellow is outlawed, and I will give ten pounds reward for his head severed from his body, and forty shillings if brought alive.'

From one of the North Carolina newspapers.

'Ran away last November, from the subscribers, a negro fellow, named Yeb; aged thirty-six. As he is outlawed, I will pay twenty pounds currency to any person who shall produce his head severed from his body, and five pounds if brought home alive. John Mosely.'

I am, gentlemen,
Your very humble servant.

Letter to the Authors of the Monthly Review,
November 30, 1774.

REFLECTIONS ON SEEING SLAVE-SHIPS AT LIVERPOOL

I preached, about noon, at Warrington; and in the evening at Liverpool, where many large ships are now laid up in the docks, which had been employed, for many years, in buying or stealing poor Africans, and selling them in America, for slaves. The men-butchers have now nothing to do at this laudable occupation; since the American war broke out, there is no demand for human cattle; so the men of Africa, as well as Europe, may enjoy their native liberty.

Journal, April 14, 1777.

WESLEY WORKS FOR THE CAUSE

MY DEAR BROTHER,

Whatever assistance I can give those generous men who join to oppose that execrable trade I certainly shall give.

I have printed a large edition of the *Thoughts upon Slavery*, and dispersed them to every part of England. But there will be vehement opposition made, both by slave-merchants and slave-holders; and they are mighty men. But our comfort is, He that dwelleth on high is mightier.

I am,

Your affectionate brother.

Letter to Thomas Funnell, November 24, 1787.

SUPPORT FOR THE ABOLITIONISTS

August, 1787.

Mr. Wesley informed the Committee of the great satisfaction which he also had experienced when he heard of their formation. He conceived that their design, while it would destroy the slave trade, would also strike at the root of the shocking abomination of slavery. He desired to forewarn them that they must expect difficulties and great opposition from those who were interested in the system, that they were a powerful body, and that they would raise all their forces when they perceived their craft to be in danger. They would employ hireling writers, who would have neither justice nor mercy. But the Committee were not to be dismayed by such treatment, nor even if some of those who professed goodwill toward them should turn against them. As to himself, he would do all he could to promote the object of their institution. He would reprint a new large edition of his *Thoughts upon Slavery*, and circulate it among his friends in England and Ireland, to whom he would add a few words in favour of their design. And then he concluded in these words: 'I commend you to Him who is able to carry you through all opposition and support you under all discouragements.'

Thomas Clarkson : History of the Abolition of the Slave Trade.

(At a meeting of the Abolition Committee on August 27, 1787, Clarkson reported that he had letters from two celebrated persons, the second from Mr. John Wesley, 'whose useful labours as a Minister of the Gospel are so well known to our countrymen'.)

SIR,

Ever since I heard of it first I felt a perfect detestation
of the horrid Slave Trade, but more particularly since I had
the pleasure of reading what you have published upon the
subject. Therefore I cannot but do everything in my power
to forward the glorious design of your Society. And it must
be a comfortable thing to every man of humanity to observe
the spirit with which you have hitherto gone on. Indeed,
you cannot go on without more than common resolution,
considering the opposition you have to encounter, all the
opposition which can be made by men who are not encum-
bered with either honour, conscience, or humanity, and
will rush on *per fasque ne fasque*, through every possible
means, to secure their great goddess, Interest. Unless they
are infatuated in this point also, they will spare no money
to carry their cause; and this has the weight of a thousand
arguments with the generality of men.

And you may be assured these men will lay hold on and
improve every possible objection against you. I have been
afraid lest they should raise an objection from your manner
of procuring information. To *hire* or to *pay* informers has a
bad sound and might raise great, yea insurmountable, prejudice against you. Is it not worth your consideration
whether it would not be advisable to drop this mode entirely,
and to be content with such information as you can procure
by more honourable means?

After all, I doubt the matter will turn upon this, 'Is the
Slave Trade for the interest of the nation?' And here the
multitude of sailors that perish therein will come to be
considered. In all these difficulties what a comfort it is to
consider (unfashionable as it is) that there is a God! Yea,
and that (as little as men think of it!) He has still all power
both in heaven and on earth! To Him I commend you
and your glorious Cause; and am, sir,

Your affectionate servant.

Letter to Granville Sharp, October 11, 1787.

A PATRIARCH'S BLESSING: GO ON, IN THE NAME OF GOD.
Balam, February 24, 1791

DEAR SIR,

Unless the divine power has raised you up to be as
Athanasius contra mundum, I see not how you can go through

your glorious enterprise in opposing that execrable villainy, which is the scandal of religion, of England, and of human nature. Unless God has raised you up for this very thing, you will be worn out by the opposition of men and devils. But if God be for you who can be against you ? Are all of them together stronger than God? O be not weary of well doing! Go on, in the name of God and in the power of His might, till even American slavery (the vilest that ever saw the sun) shall vanish away before it.

Reading this morning a tract wrote by a poor African, I was particularly struck by that circumstance, that a man who has a black skin, being wronged or outraged by a white man, can have no redress; it being a *law* in all our Colonies that the *oath* of a black against a white goes for nothing. What villainy is this!

That He who has guided you from youth up may continue to strengthen you in this and all things is the prayer of, dear sir,

Your affectionate servant.

Letter to William Wilberforce, February 24, 1791.

(The last letter Wesley ever wrote, written after reading the life of a negro slave called Gustavus Vasa, and on hearing that Wilberforce had expressed himself despondently about the prospects of the cause.)

"We dedicate, therefore, our citizenship to the service of Christ and humanity, to the end that freedom and justice, virtue and neighbourly regard, goodwill and peace, may be established on the earth.'

This should mean 20,000 'cells' of daring and experimental Christian living on the private and social planes.   You should be one of them.

10. Wesley's followers can never stand still. Under God he raised up a community which is driven by the Holy Spirit to new thinking and action and prayer and consequent grace. It is said of Wesley that he was a man centuries ahead of his time. The mark of a Methodist to-day is that he should be centuries ahead of his.

11. Nor is the Methodist Church of Great Britain alone in this work. There is a great stirring throughout the universal Church of Christ.   This July (1937) nearly a thousand delegates from every non-Roman Church and almost every land met together for a fortnight at Oxford in a great ecumenical Conference to grapple together with these problems of economic and international anarchy. These disorders have for years challenged the Church and men have not been slow to point out the ineffectiveness of the Church's response.

But now the Church has challenged itself and the world in the name of Jesus Christ. It has sent out a message to the Christian Churches, and with this great message, in which the followers of John Wesley joined, which points the way to the future, we conclude this book.

A MESSAGE FROM THE OXFORD CONFERENCE TO THE CHRISTIAN CHURCHES

The delegates to the World Conference on Church, Community and State, assembled at Oxford from July 12 to 26, 1937, send at the close of their deliberations the following message to the Churches of Christ throughout the world:—

In the name of Christ, greetings.

We meet at a time when mankind is oppressed with perplexity and fear. Men are burdened with evils almost insupportable and with problems apparently insoluble. Even in countries which are at peace, unemployment and malnutrition sap men's strength of body, mind and spirit. In other countries war does its devil's work, and threatens to overwhelm us all in its limitless catastrophe.

Yet we do not take up our task as bewildered citizens of our several nations, asking if anywhere there is a clue to our problems; we take it up as Christians, to whom is committed 'the word of reconciliation', that 'God was in Christ reconciling the world unto Himself'.

The first duty of the Church and its greatest service to the world is that it be in very deed the Church—confessing the true faith, committed to the fulfilment of the will of Christ, its only Lord, and united in Him in a fellowship of love and service.

We do not call the world to be like ourselves, for we are already too like the world. Only as we ourselves repent, both as individuals and as corporate bodies, can the Church call men to repentance. The call to ourselves and to the world is to Christ.

Despite our unfaithfulness God has done great things through His Church. One of the greatest is this—that, notwithstanding the tragedy of our divisions and our inability in many important matters to speak with a united voice, there exists an actual world-fellowship. Our unity in Christ is not a theme for aspiration; it is an experienced fact. We can speak of it with boldness because our Conference is an illustration of it. We are drawn from many nations and from many different communions, from Churches with centuries of history behind them and from the younger Churches whose story covers but a few decades; but we are one in Christ.

The unity of this fellowship is not built up from its constituent parts, like a federation of different States. It consists in the Sovereignty and redeeming acts of its one Lord. The source of unity is not the consenting movement of men's wills; it is Jesus Christ whose one life flows through the Body and subdues the many wills to His.

The Christian sees distinctions of race as part of God's purpose to enrich mankind with a diversity of gifts. Against racial pride or race-antagonism the Church must set its face implacably as rebellion against God. Especially in its own life and worship, there can be no place for barriers because of race or colour. Similarly, the Christian accepts national communities as part of God's purpose to enrich and diversify human life. Every man is called of God to serve his fellows in the community to which he belongs. But national egotism tending to the suppression of other nationalities or of minorities is, no less than individual egotism, a sin against the Creator of all peoples and races. The deification of nation, race or class, or of political or cultural ideals, is idolatry, and can only lead to increasing division and disaster.

On every side we see men seeking for a life of fellowship in which they experience their dependence on one another. But because community is sought on a wrong basis, the intensity of the search for it issues in conflict and disintegration. In such a world the Church is called to be in its own life that fellowship which binds men together in their common dependence on God and overleaps all barriers of social status, race or nationality.

In consonance with its nature as true community, the Church will call the nations to order their lives as members of the one family of God. The universal Church surveying the nations of the world, in every one of which it is now planted and rooted, must pronounce a condemnation of war unqualified and unrestricted. War can occur only as a fruit and manifestation of sin. This truth is unaffected by any question what may be the duty of a nation which has to choose between entry upon war and a course which it believes to be a betrayal of right, or what may be the duty of a Christian citizen whose country is involved in war. The condemnation of war stands, and also the obligation to seek the way of freeing mankind from its physical, moral and spiritual ravages. If war breaks out, then pre-eminently the Church must manifestly be the Church, still united as the one Body of Christ, though the nations wherein it is planted fight each other, consciously offering the same prayers that God's Name may be hallowed, His Kingdom come, and His Will be done in both, or all, the warring nations. This fellowship of prayer must at all costs remain unbroken. The Church must also hold together in one spiritual fellowship those of its members who take different views concerning their duty as Christian citizens in time of war.

To condemn war is not enough. Many situations conceal the fact of conflict under the guise of outward peace. Christians must do all in their power to promote among the nations justice and peaceful co-operation, and the means of peaceful adjustment to altering conditions. Especially should Christians in more fortunate countries press the demand for justice on behalf of the less fortunate. The insistence upon justice must express itself in a demand for such mitigation of the sovereignty of national States as is involved in the abandonment by each of the claim to be judge in its own cause.

We recognize the State as being in its own sphere the highest authority. It has the God-given aim in that sphere to uphold law and order and to minister to the life of its people. But as all authority is from God, the State stands under His judgement. God is Himself the source of justice, of which the State is not lord but servant. The Christian can acknowledge no ultimate authority but God; his loyalty to the State is part of his loyalty to God and must never usurp the place of that primary and only absolute loyalty.

The Church has duties laid upon it by God, which at all cost it must perform, among which the chief is to proclaim the Word of God and to make disciples, and to order its own life in the power of the Spirit dwelling in it. Because this is its duty it must do it, whether or not the State consents;

and the State on its side should recognize the duty and assure full liberty for its performance. The Church can claim such liberty for itself only as it is also concerned for the rights and liberties of others.

In the economic sphere the first duty of the Church is to insist that economic activities, like every other department of human life, stand under the judgement of Christ. The existence of economic classes presents a barrier to human fellowship which cannot be tolerated by the Christian conscience. Indefensible inequalities of opportunity in regard to education, leisure, and health continue to prevail. The ordering of economic life has tended to enhance acquisitiveness and to set up a false standard of economic and social success. The only forms of employment open to many men and women, or the fact that none is open, prevent them from finding a sense of Christian vocation in their daily life.

We are witnessing new movements which have arisen in reaction to these evils but which combine with their struggle for social justice the repudiation of all religious faith. Aware of the reality of sin, the Church knows that no change in the outward ordering of life can of itself eradicate social evil. The Church therefore cannot surrender to the utopian expectations of these movements, and their godlessness it must unequivocally reject; but in doing so it must recognize that Christians in their blindness to the challenging evils of the economic order have been partly responsible for the anti-religious character of these movements.

Christians have a double duty—both to bear witness to their faith within the existing economic order and also to test all economic institutions in the light of their understanding of God's will. The forces of evil against which Christians have to contend are found not only in the hearts of men as individuals, but have entered into and infected the structure of society and there also must be combated. The responsibility of the Church is to insist on the true relationship of spiritual and economic goods. Man cannot live without bread, and man cannot live by bread alone. Our human wealth consists in fellowship with God and in Him with our brethren. To this fellowship the whole economic order must be made subservient.

The questions which have mainly engaged the attention of the Conference are questions that can be effectively dealt with, in practice, only by the laity. Those who are responsible for the daily conduct of industry, administration and public life must discover for themselves what is the right decision in an endless variety of concrete situations. If they are to receive the help they need in making responsible Christian decisions new types of ministry will have to be developed by the Church.

The fulfilment of the tasks to which the Church is called to-day lies largely in the hands of youth. Many loud voices are calling on young people to give themselves to political and social ideals, and it is often hard for them to hear the voice of Jesus Christ who calls them to be servants of the eternal Kingdom. Yet many of the younger generation, often in spite of ridicule and sometimes of persecution, are turning to Him, and individually as well as in Christian youth movements devote themselves to the renewal of the life of the Churches and to making known the Good News of Christ by word and action. We rejoice in their brave witness.

In the education of youth the Church has a twofold task. First, it must be eager to secure for every citizen the fullest possible opportunity for the development of the gifts that God has bestowed on him. In particular, the Church must condemn inequality of educational opportunity as a main obstacle to fulness of fellowship in the life of the community.

While the Church is thus concerned with all education it has, also, a special responsibility to realize its own understanding of the meaning and end of education in the relation of life to God. In education, as elsewhere, if God is not recognized, He is ignored. The Church must claim the liberty to give a Christian education to its own children. It is in the field of education that the conflict between Christian faith and non-Christian conceptions of the ends of life, between the Church and an all-embracing community life which claims to be the source and goal of every human activity, is in many parts of the world most acute. In this conflict all is at stake, and the Church must gird itself for the struggle.

As we look to the future it is our hope and prayer that the Spirit of God may cause new life to break forth spontaneously in a multitude of different centres, and that there may come into being a large number of 'cells' of Christian men and women associated in small groups for the discovery of fresh ways in which they may serve God and their fellow-men.

We have deeply felt the absence from our fellowship of the Churches that have not been represented at the Conference. Our hearts are filled with anguish as we remember the suffering of the Church in Russia. Our sympathy and gratitude go out to our Christian brethren in Germany; we are moved to a more living trust by their steadfast witness to Christ and we pray that we may be given grace to bear the same clear witness to the Lord.

We have much to encourage us since the Conference at Stockholm twelve years ago. The sense of the unity of the Church in all the world grows stronger every year. We trust that this cause will be yet more fully served by the World Council of Churches, proposals for which have been considered by the Conference and commended to the Churches.

We have tried during these days at Oxford to look without illusion at the chaos and disintegration of the world, the injustices of the social order and the menace and horror of war. The world is anxious and bewildered and full of pain and fear. We are troubled yet we do not despair. Our hope is anchored in the living God. In Christ, and in the union of man with God and of man with man, which He creates, life even in face of all these evils has a meaning. In His Name we set our hands, as the servants of God and in Him of one another, to the task of proclaiming God's message of redemption, of living as His children and of combating injustice, cruelty and hate. The Church can be of good cheer; it hears its Lord saying, 'I have overcome the world'.

INDEX OF SOURCES